SpringerBriefs in Applied Sciences and Technology

SpringerBriefs present concise summaries of cutting-edge research and practical applications across a wide spectrum of fields. Featuring compact volumes of 50 to 125 pages, the series covers a range of content from professional to academic.

Typical publications can be:

- A timely report of state-of-the art methods
- An introduction to or a manual for the application of mathematical or computer techniques
- A bridge between new research results, as published in journal articles
- A snapshot of a hot or emerging topic
- An in-depth case study
- A presentation of core concepts that students must understand in order to make independent contributions

SpringerBriefs are characterized by fast, global electronic dissemination, standard publishing contracts, standardized manuscript preparation and formatting guidelines, and expedited production schedules.

On the one hand, **SpringerBriefs in Applied Sciences and Technology** are devoted to the publication of fundamentals and applications within the different classical engineering disciplines as well as in interdisciplinary fields that recently emerged between these areas. On the other hand, as the boundary separating fundamental research and applied technology is more and more dissolving, this series is particularly open to trans-disciplinary topics between fundamental science and engineering.

Indexed by EI-Compendex, SCOPUS and Springerlink.

Azman Ismail · Fatin Nur Zulkipli ·
Husna Sarirah Husin · Andreas Öchsner
Editors

Emerging Technologies and Sustainable Solutions

Exploring Innovations Across Industries

Editors
Azman Ismail
Maritime Engineering Technology
Malaysian Institute of Marine Engineering
Technology, Universiti Kuala Lumpur
Lumut, Perak, Malaysia

Husna Sarirah Husin
Taylor's University
Subang Jaya, Selangor, Malaysia

Fatin Nur Zulkipli
College of Computing,
Informatics and Mathematics
Universiti Teknologi MARA
Machang, Kelantan, Malaysia

Andreas Öchsner
Faculty of Mechanical Engineering
Esslingen University of Applied Sciences
Esslingen, Baden-Württemberg, Germany

ISSN 2191-530X ISSN 2191-5318 (electronic)
SpringerBriefs in Applied Sciences and Technology
ISBN 978-3-032-18180-0 ISBN 978-3-032-18181-7 (eBook)
https://doi.org/10.1007/978-3-032-18181-7

This Springer imprint is published by the registered company Springer Nature Switzerland AG
The registered company address is: Gewerbestrasse 11, 6330 Cham, Switzerland

Preface

This book offers a comprehensive journey through 15 chapters, each illuminating a distinct aspect of technological advancement and its impact on sustainability. From IoT-driven aquaponics systems to predictive maintenance models, the book traverses diverse domains such as maritime leadership, data analysis, health care, and environmental management. Through practical insights and theoretical frameworks, it unveils how cutting-edge technologies like blockchain, AI, and IoT are revolutionizing traditional practices, fostering sustainability, and enhancing societal well-being. By navigating through real-world applications and challenges, this book can serve as a guide for researchers, practitioners, and policymakers, showcasing the transformative potential of technology in building a more sustainable future.

Lumut, Malysia | Azman Ismail
Machang, Malaysia | Fatin Nur Zulkipli
Subang Jaya, Malaysia | Husna Sarirah Husin
Esslingen, Germany | Andreas Öchsner

Contents

Chapter 1
Design of an IoT-Based Aquaponics System with Monitoring Capabilities

Suzanna Samsudin, Noratikah Zawani Mahabob, and Che Munira Che Razali

Abstract The increased quality of life in recent times has led to a tremendous growth in research on IoT technology systems. This paper's goal is to provide an IoT-based aquaponics system with monitoring capabilities that uses a NodeMCU ESP32 microcontroller board to enable remote control and Blynk application-based electrical device monitoring. In order to read and measure the pH value and the percentage of water level, this system used sensors such as pH and water level sensors. Hydroponic and aquaculture systems are combined to create the aquaponics system prototype. Air is used as a growth medium for plants in hydroponic gardening. Fish are raised or cultivated using an aquaculture system. With this novel technique, water is sent from the hydroponic system to the aquaculture, and air is returned to the hydroponic system from the aquaculture. Fish waste that is beneficial to plants can be found in aquaculture water.

Keywords IoT · Aquaponics · Hydroponics

1.1 Introduction

The term aquaponics describes the system that enables the simultaneous practice of hydroponics (growing plants without soil) and aquaculture (raising fish). The nitrifying bacteria transform the fish excretions, which contain ammonia, into nitrites and subsequently nitrates, which the plants can utilize as nutrients. When compared

S. Samsudin (✉) · N. Z. Mahabob · C. M. C. Razali
Politeknik Ungku Omar, Ipoh, Malaysia
e-mail: suzanna@puo.edu.my

N. Z. Mahabob
e-mail: noratikahzawani@puo.edu.my

C. M. C. Razali
e-mail: chemunira@puo.edu.my

A. Ismail et al. (eds.), *Emerging Technologies and Sustainable Solutions*, SpringerBriefs in Applied Sciences and Technology,
https://doi.org/10.1007/978-3-032-18181-7_1

to conventional agricultural techniques, aquaponics works well in areas lacking in water, healthy soil, or even available land [1].

When compared to traditional plant growth methods, the aquaponics system has a number of advantages. For example, it grows faster, requires no soil, can be planted anywhere, and takes up significantly less space. Seasonal changes also have no effect on plant growth, and plants are protected from a variety of diseases. Breeding aquatic plants and animals through a variety of approaches, skills, and methods is known as aquaculture [1]. Continuous monitoring of the biological, chemical, and physical products helps to prevent degradation that could lead to the production process failing as well as forecast unfavorable conditions in aquaculture. This system allows for the monitoring of variables such as temperature, oxygen content, pH, ammonia, and others that are critical for controlling aquaculture processes. Numerous well-organized sensors, as well as other technologies that can support the system, allow wireless networks operating in the monitoring region to gather and transfer information to the controlling system. Similar to this, the hydroponic system has several controlling parameters that include the fertilizer container, water level, artificial light intensity, pH adjustment solution, ionic conductivity, etc. The Internet of Things (IoT) must be used to monitor and control the value of all these parameters. Artificial intelligence (AI), machine learning, and deep learning must also be used to correlate, process, and analyze these metrics for efficient handling [2].

Water use for agricultural crops is high these days. It takes an estimated 2000 to 5000 gallons of water each day to generate enough food for one person. In addition to using a lot of water, fertilizers—especially chemical fertilizers, which are the primary input in conventional farming methods—are used excessively, which poses a challenge for food production. In addition to contaminating the environment, particularly water resources, the usage of these chemical fertilizers is a significant factor in agricultural output costs. Realizing the value of resource conservation and environmental friendliness, aquaponics—a hybrid system combining hydroponics and aquaculture—was discovered to be able to lower the amount of water and fertilizer used in agriculture. This makes it a viable option for urban areas with constrained living spaces as well as for society at large. According to the findings, this aquaponics system can reduce agricultural land use by 75% and water consumption by up to 80%. The concept was given in a different planned publication, with a gravel media bed to rearing tank ratio of 2:1. The system consisted of three water pumps, vinyl tubing, gravel media, and timber frames with waterproof lining. The pumps served as a safety valve in case of an overflow from the aquaculture tank, as well as an intake to the hydroponic grow bed. When the system was first developed, it included 3-inch hard PVC drainpipes, which made it very inaccessible and challenging to use. To improve accessibility across the system, 1.5-inch vinyl tubing was used in place of these pipes. To stop water loss from overflow, float switches were also installed to the system. Additional applications for this technology include those in broadcast, smart cars, remote sensing, highways, and other fields [3].

Due to its similarity to natural systems, where water efficiency is significantly enhanced, and its reduced environmental impact, aquaponics is regarded as a type of sustainable agriculture [4]. The aquaponics system has successfully addressed environmental degradation and realized the transfer from waste to nutrients as a sustainable, circular, efficient, and intensive low-carbon production mode for the future. Aquaponics can help address the global food crisis and promote sustainability if it is widely adopted as a commercial option [5].

Additional research revealed that managing an aquaponics system involves three distinct concepts: fish, plants, and microorganisms. As a result, the topic is highly complex. The entire system could be in danger if a specific water quality parameter is not maintained, especially the pH stabilization, which could result in the mass extinction of beneficial bacteria, plants, and fish. Most plant species generally require a pH of between 6 and 6.5 to improve nutrient uptake [6]. In contrast, fish require a pH range of 7–9 in order to grow as efficiently as possible [7]. A high pH (> 7) is necessary for the nitrifying bacteria. As a result, the optimal pH range for the entire aquaponics system is 6.0–8.0. In order to stabilize the water quality parameters in this aquaponics system, maintaining this pH range is very important [8, 9].

This paper proposes to create an IoT-based automated aquaponics monitoring system using a NodeMCU ESP32 and the Blynk app through WiFi, based on the previous discussion. The suggested design is simple to use and implement.

1.2 Methodology

1.2.1 Block Diagram

Figure 1.1 illustrates the overall block diagram of an IoT-based automated aquaponics system. Within the input section, the pH and water level sensors serve as input components, providing information to the controller. The Blynk software utilizes WiFi for data transfer to the server, enabling control of the output components. Additionally, the 5 V adapter, supplying the system's input power, is included in the input section. The NodeMCU ESP32 microcontroller board processes input signals from the input components to generate output signals in the process section. Through WiFi, a signal can be transmitted to the NodeMCU ESP32 to regulate the pH and water level in an aquarium, or it can be received by the Blynk server. The pump receives signals from the microcontroller. The aquarium's pH and water level are viewable through the Blynk app. To verify WiFi connectivity, connect the NodeMCU ESP32 to WiFi and open the Arduino IDE. Upon activation, the pH and water level sensors will proceed to measure the pH and water level, respectively. The collected data will then be transmitted to the microcontroller. The Blynk application facilitates the visualization and monitoring of all incoming data. If the water level drops below 50%, the Blynk application will alert users with the message "water is drain water pump on!" triggering the automatic activation of the water pump. The water pump will deactivate if the water level exceeds 50%. Refer to Fig. 1.2 for the system operating flowchart.

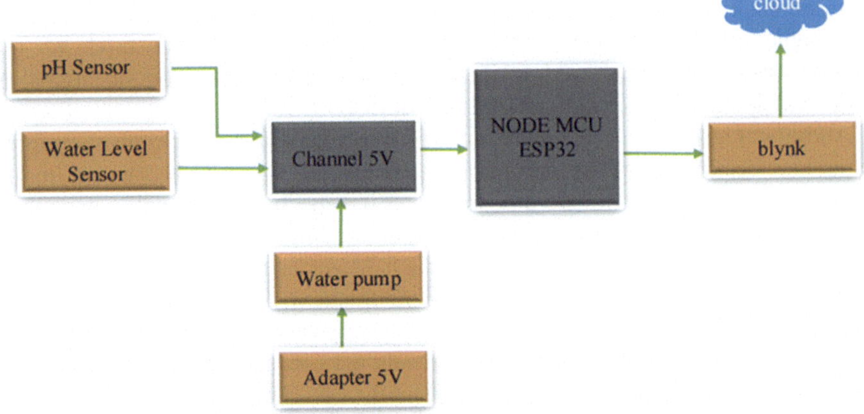

Fig. 1.1 Block diagram of the IoT-based aquaponics system

1.2.2 Project Hardware and Software

Table 1.1 outlines the hardware and software to be used for the project. The software utilized in this project includes the Blynk IoT app and the Arduino IDE. The Blynk IoT app and website are employed for creating a template to enable remote control of the devices from a smartphone. Meanwhile, the Arduino IDE is utilized for coding and uploading the program into the microcontroller for the project.

1.2.3 Prototype Development

Figures 1.3 and 1.4 depict the prototype of the project's system and the schematic circuit that has been constructed.

1.3 Results and Discussion

1.3.1 Testing and Evaluation

The design prototype was tested by evaluating its components and modules. Following this, the sensor was tested with various water types to establish measurable readings, including determining the maximum and minimum pH values for the project. The reading will appear on the Blynk app as shown in Fig. 1.5. Initially, the sensor's measurement will show significant differences. Therefore, we need to wait for at least 3 to 5 min to obtain an accurate reading.

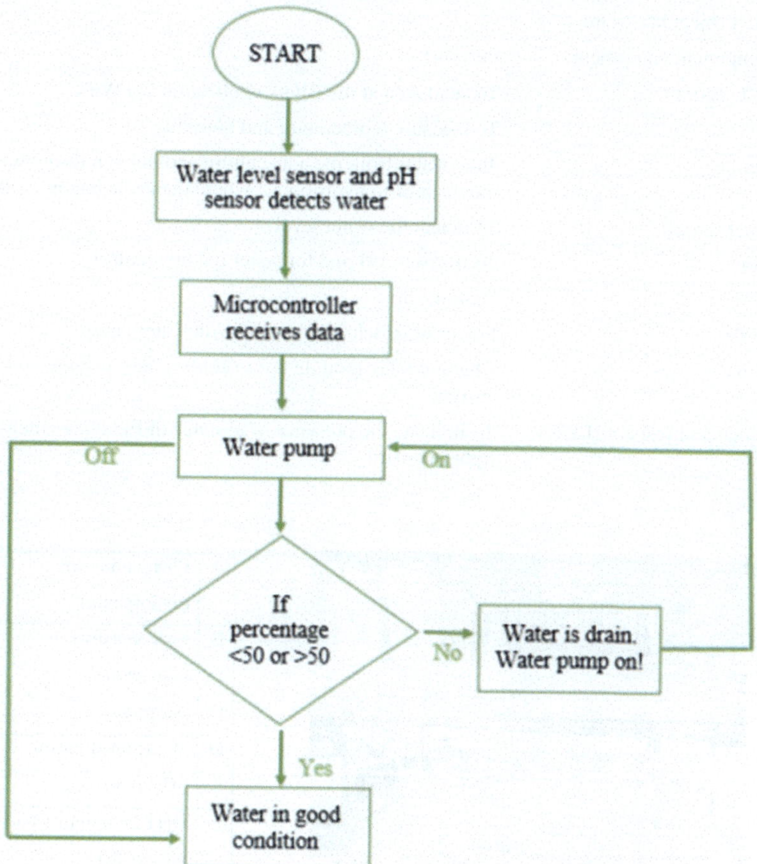

Fig. 1.2 Flowchart of the system

The project underwent testing to determine the readability of data transmitted using NodeMCU ESP32. The pH sensor and water level sensor are responsible for measuring pH and water levels. Subsequently, the microcontroller will receive the collected data, all of which can be monitored on the Blynk app. If the water level falls below 50%, the Blynk application will send notifications stating "water is draining, water pump on!" and the water pump will automatically activate. When the water level exceeds 50%, the water pump will turn off and the Blynk application will display "water in good condition." Consequently, the readings transmitted by NodeMCU ESP32 will be received by the Blynk app, and the values will be displayed.

Table 1.1 Project hardware

Items/component/equipment	Purpose
NodeMCU ESP32	To send data at the Blynk application via WiFi
DHT22	To measure temperature and humidity
Water pump	Take water from the aquaculture and move it through the motor back to hydroponic, where the cycle begins again
Water level sensor	To detect the water level
pH sensor	To measure pH and for water quality control
Air pump	Push the air
Adapter 5V	Power input which connects with water pump
Channel 5V	Channel relay module use to control high voltage and high current
Light-dependent resistor (LDR)	To indicate the presence or absence of light or to measure light intensity

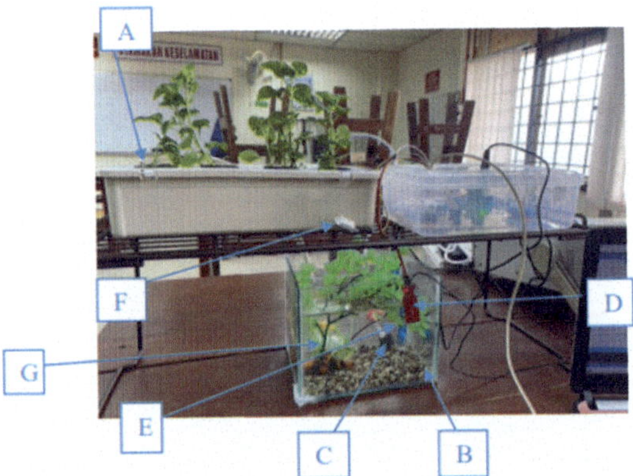

A	Plant container (hydroponic)
B	Fish container (aquaculture)
C	Air pump
D	Water level sensor
E	pH sensor
F	DHT22 humidity and temperature
G	Water pump

Fig. 1.3 Prototype of the IoT-based aquaponics system

1.3.2 Discussion

The IoT-based automated prototype for an aquaponics system runs well because fish waste has supplied the plant with nutrients and the plant has filtered the fish water, and water usage can be maximized. Sensors in both systems take measurements of a crucial parameter. It can be shown on the user dashboard for monitoring reasons with these parameters. Real-time data analytics is displayed for all significant metrics as they are gathered from the sensor and transmitted via the ESP32 module via the internet. The manufacturing line, which will have a more organized schedule for moving the product for smart agriculture, will benefit greatly from this research.

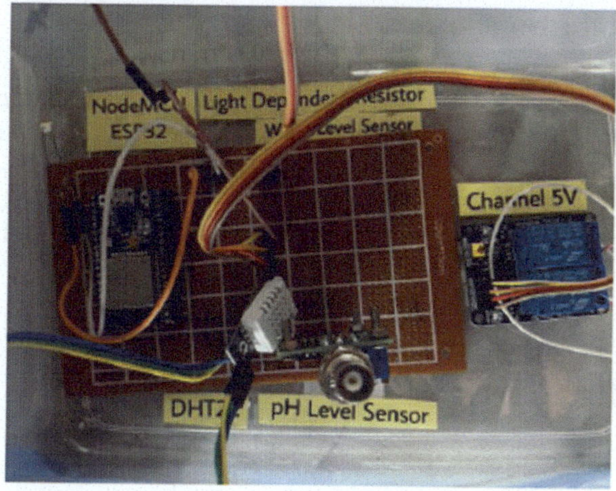

Fig. 1.4 Prototype of the schematic circuit

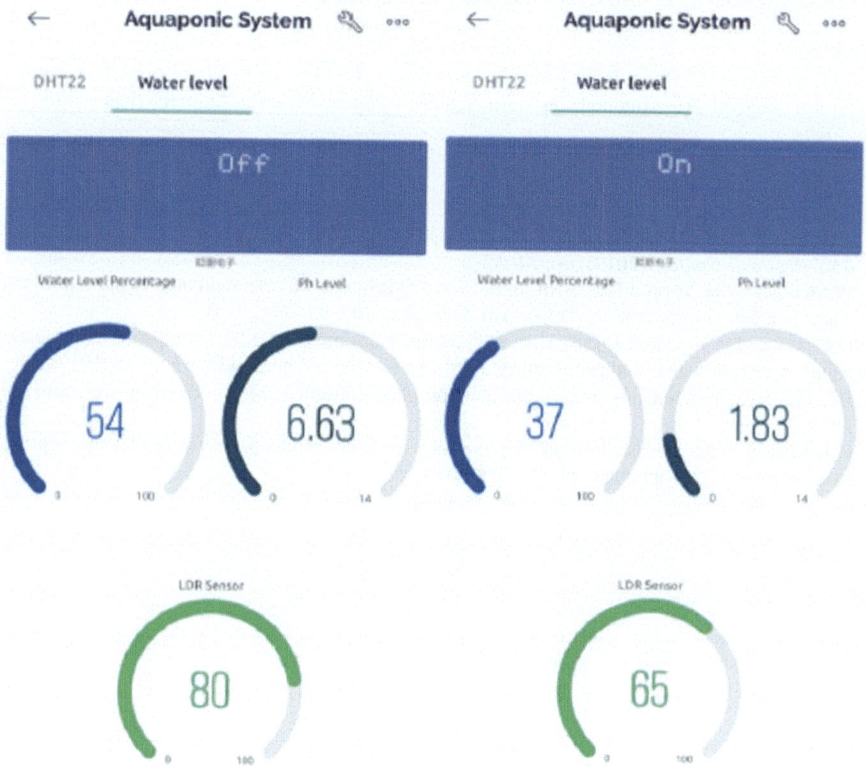

Fig. 1.5 pH and water level percentage displayed in Blynk app

1.4 Conclusion

This suggested IoT-based automated aquaponics system was developed using the NodeMCU ESP 32 and the Blynk IoT application. An Internet-connected smartphone is used to operate this system. It is believed that this project will assist the community in addressing its water scarcity. The community has benefited greatly from this project's ability to transmit data and information online in order to monitor and maintain the cleanliness of the water.

References

1. M.F. Perla, A.J. Oscar, R.G. Enrique, et al.: Perspective for aquaponic systems: Omic technologies for microbial community analysis. BioMed. Res. Int. Article id 480386 (2019)
2. E. Elia, C. Hodoşan, L. Nistor, F. Dumitrache, N.A. Savidov.: System cycling stage on aquaponic systems as required prerequisite for soilless agriculture. Sci. Pap.: Ser. D, Anim. Sci. 381–384 (2020)
3. C.G. Nichols, D.C. Popa, R.A. Turek, F. Dumitrache, D. Mocuţa, E. Elia: Lowtech aquaponic system based on an ornamental aquarium. Scientific Papers: Series D, Animal Science, 385–390 (2020)
4. Frost: smart aquaponics system: challenges and opportunities. Eur. J. Adv. Eng. Technol. 52–55 (2019)
5. A.K. Ng, Y.K. Lim, H.S. Tay, W.S. Kwang, S.R. Hettiarachchi.: A smart recirculating aquaculture system with NI compact RIO and WSN. *Proceedings of NI Engineering Impact Awards ASEAN/ ANZ Regional Contest* (2019), pp. 24–32
6. W.M. Lewis, J.H. Yopp, J.H.L. Schramm, Use of hydroponics to maintain quality of recirculated water in a fish culture system. Trans. Am. Fish. Soc. **107**, 92–99 (2019)
7. D.C. Love, J.P. Fry, X. Li, E.S. Hill, J. Genello, K. Semmens, R.E. Thompson, Commercial aquaponics production and profitability. Find. An Int. Surv. Aquac. **435**, 67–74 (2019)
8. J.E. Rakocy, Aquaponics—integrating fish and plant culture. J. Agric., Environ. Consum. Sci. **19**, 5–13 (2019)
9. R.J. Sutton, W.M. Lewis.: Further observations on a fish production system that incorporates hydroponically grown plants. **44**, 55–59 (2019)

Chapter 2
Maritime Leadership Module Using a Ship Navigation Simulator

Zulkifly Mat Radzi, Mohd Najib Abdul Ghani Yolhamid, Nanthini Sridewi Appan, and Mohamad Azrin Abd Azis

Abstract The research problem revealed that maritime operation students need to be trained in leadership to be a competent graduate officer for the maritime agencies and industry. For example, the competency for the naval cadet officers will be based on the characteristics of leaders in the Royal Malaysian Navy. The students will be assessed on the leadership skill to perform the duties of an Officer of the Watch, teamwork to achieve the mission, communication skill, making correct decision for safety in navigation, critical thinking process, command, and control on board a ship. The maritime leadership module shall be conducted in the ship navigation simulator to reduce operational costs, due to limited training availability on board ship and to ensure a systematic training methodology.

Keywords Leadership · Module · Simulator · Training · Assessment

2.1 Introduction

Malaysia's Ministry of Higher Education announced the Malaysia Education Blueprint 2015–2025, which defined ways to attain excellence in the education system among institutions of higher learning [1]. The blueprint sets a direction for the improvement of students with strong moral values, relevant knowledge in their

Z. M. Radzi (✉) · M. N. A. G. Yolhamid · N. S. Appan · M. A. A. Azis
National Defence University of Malaysia, Kuala Lumpur, Malaysia
e-mail: zulkifly@upnm.edu.my

M. N. A. G. Yolhamid
e-mail: najib@upnm.edu.my

N. S. Appan
e-mail: nanthini@upnm.edu.my

M. A. A. Azis
e-mail: m.azrin@upnm.edu.my

A. Ismail et al. (eds.), *Emerging Technologies and Sustainable Solutions*, SpringerBriefs in Applied Sciences and Technology,
https://doi.org/10.1007/978-3-032-18181-7_2

disciplines, sound mindsets, and good behaviors, aligning with the nation's educational philosophy. Graduates possessing these qualities contribute to the battlement of families, society, the nation, and the world community. The aim of this paper is to implement the maritime leadership module (MLM), which consists of leadership competency in officer of the watch (OOW), teamwork to achieve the mission, communication skill, making correct decisions for safety in navigation, critical thinking process, and command and control using a ship navigation simulator.

The leadership of maritime operation students focuses on the concept of developing officers and gentlemen with attitude and politeness according to the National Education Philosophy [1]. The development of graduates' officer needs to be emphasized at the early stage of students' life. The academic results alone are not enough to produce the right leadership because building a strong personality and good behavior are necessary components to prepare graduates for their future employment onboard ships. Therefore, the performance of students cannot be solely based on academic achievements alone. Accepting leadership characteristics is one of the attributes of a graduate officer that must be evaluated before a student graduates. Values that must be fostered include a positive attitude, ethics, morale, good virtues, tenacity, good manners, and discipline. Thus, graduates play a crucial role in instilling civility and other good behavior in students, transforming them into officers and gentlemen [2].

2.2 Methodology

The development of MLM was based on the application of the ADDIE model [3] as shown in Fig. 2.1. To support the framework of leadership development of maritime graduates, the MLM program incorporates the use of a ship navigation simulator. The simulator can create real situations at sea, allowing students to exercise leadership practices onboard a ship [4]. The lecturer will develop the graduate leadership which contains objective, schedules, tasks, frequencies, evaluations, and assessments of learning outcomes.

During the MLM, students will engage in team-based interactions to navigate the ship toward a certain destination and encourage their leadership development [5]. They will take turns assuming the roles of leader and team member. The program incorporates interactive elements like team building exercises and navigation simulators to develop students' leadership skills. Giving students hands-on experience, such as acting as the officer of the watch (OOW) in a simulated environment, not only helps them understand the practical aspects of their future roles but also fosters confidence and decision-making abilities. The combination of theoretical knowledge and practical application is likely to prepare students well for their future careers in maritime operations [6]. The navigation simulator effectively addresses the psychomotor domain by providing students with hands-on experience in operating radar systems, Electronic Chart Display and Information Systems (ECDIS), Global Positioning System (GPS), Global Maritime Distress and Safety System (GMDSS), the ship's wheel, engine throttle controls, and other navigation devices integrated

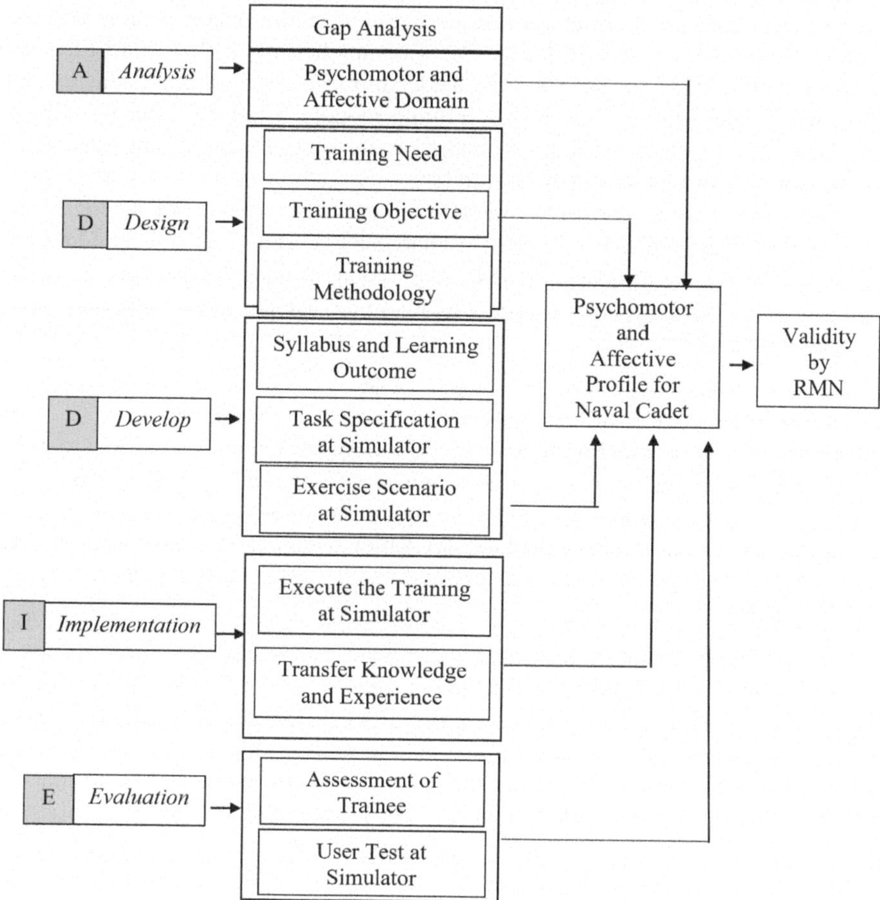

Fig. 2.1 Application of ADDIE model for MLM using ship navigation simulator [3]

into the simulator [7]. Simulated maritime training provides a crucial link between theoretical knowledge and real-world application. It is like a rehearsal before the main performance, giving students the chance to apply what they have learned in a classroom. This approach not only enhances their understanding of theoretical concepts but also builds practical skills that will be invaluable when they step into actual on-the-job situations. It is a smart way to ensure that students are well-prepared and confident before embarking on their maritime careers.

Using a simulator for psychomotor training is an effective way to transfer knowledge and experience [8]. It not only helps students develop practical skills but also exposes them to modern technologies used in the field. The incorporation of information and communication technology adds a contemporary edge to their training, aligning them with industry advancements. It is impressive how the training covers psychomotor and affective domains, ensuring a well-rounded development of skills and attitudes. And the facilitator's role in assessing performance ensures that the training objectives are met. It seems like a comprehensive and forward-thinking approach to preparing the students for leadership roles in maritime agencies and industries. Implementing a leadership training module within the ship navigation simulator aims to equip students with the necessary leadership competencies to perform the role of OOW onboard a ship [7].

Developing assessment rubrics aligned with industry needs is crucial for evaluating students' performance as leaders of character [1]. These rubrics should reflect the specific leadership qualities and skills required in the maritime industry. Here are some potential learning outcomes for students in the leadership module at the ship navigation simulator:

a. Leadership skills to perform the duty as OOW.
b. Ability to organize a ship navigation team to achieve the mission.
c. Ability to communicate with members of navigation team.
d. Ability in making correct decisions as a leader for the safety in navigation.
e. Ability in critical thinking of appreciating the situation to avoid a collision.
f. Ability to command and control the navigation team to achieve the mission.
g. Ability to work in a team as a leader and instill moral courage in the members of the team.

The evaluation must indicate the grade, value point, and marks that will be awarded for the student's performance. The facilitators are in charge of evaluating the students during their competency assessments on the ship navigation simulator. Prior to the evaluation, students will complete training modules in the ship navigation simulator, covering the five levels of affective learning. When assessing a student's performance, the lecturer must apply conventional rubrics. The lecturer will utilize rubrics to assign grades to the students. Table 2.1 shows the rubrics for the student's assessment.

Validity is a researcher's capacity to accurately quantify the usefulness of an operational concept in a subject matter [9]. Student leadership should be evaluated based on their ability to complete a task effectively. To confirm the legitimacy of the student's assessment, engage an external validator and subject matter expert in MLM. For example, RMN top management officers were invited to evaluate the naval cadet's performances. The student's task shall align with the RMN leadership standards.

2.3 Results and Discussion

A pilot test was then carried out to ensure the applicability and practicality of the navy cadet leadership module in the ship navigation simulator. The objectives include ensuring the training module's applicability, limiting the number of students per session, establishing evaluation criteria, and determining the method for assigning marks to students. Conducting a pilot test involving sixty students from the bachelor's degree in maritime technology program, along with two facilitators who are

Table 2.1 Rubrics for maritime leadership module assessment

Grading	Mark	Description
Excellence	10	Having very high leadership ability in doing the task. The performance is always above the maximum requirement
	9	Having very high leadership ability in doing the task. The performance is above the maximum requirement
Good	8	Having high leadership ability in doing the task. The performance is always at the maximum requirement
	7	Having high leadership ability in doing the task. The performance is at the maximum requirement
Satisfactory	6	Having moderate leadership ability in doing the task. The performance is always above the minimum requirement
	5	Having moderate leadership ability in doing the task. The performance is above the minimum requirement
Weak	4	Having low leadership ability in doing the task. The performance is at the minimum requirement
	3	Having low leadership ability in doing the task. The performances are always at the minimum requirement
Poor	2	Having very low leadership ability in doing the task. The performance is below the minimum requirement
	1	Having very low leadership ability in doing the task. The performance is always below minimum requirement

navigation science lecturers, is a significant step in assessing the effectiveness of the leadership training module at the ship navigation simulator.

It is common for pilot tests to uncover areas where students may face challenges, especially when transitioning from simulated environments to real-world scenarios. The identification of tasks that were found to be challenging due to students' lack of experience in actual shipboard operations is valuable feedback. The assessment criteria used were effective in measuring the leadership traits of the students. The scale ranging from 0 to 10 is suitable to be used to evaluate the students' performance.

The results of the naval cadet leadership module indicate a mixed performance among students, with 35% passing with a grade of B and 55% passing with 60% or below. Despite the variation in grades, these results are considered acceptable given that the passing grade for all subjects in the bachelor's degree program is set at 40% or a grade of D+. The leadership module conducted using the ship navigation simulator was effective and well received. The decision to limit the number of students per session to ten ensures a manageable group size for effective facilitation and individualized attention. Having three facilitators allows for diverse perspectives and expertise in assessing students' leadership traits, contributing to a comprehensive evaluation process. The reliability of the rubrics used further strengthens the credibility of the assessment, ensuring consistency and fairness in evaluating students' leadership abilities. Overall, the results indicate that the leadership module conducted with the ship navigation simulator is suitable for training naval cadets, and the assessment methods employed are robust and reliable. This positive feedback underscores the value of incorporating simulation-based training in leadership development programs.

The facilitator of the MLM is responsible for assessing the leadership trait. The assessment occurs at the end of the semester, when the module has been completed. The lecturer teaching navigation is responsible for facilitating MLM for maritime students. This MLM will be implemented during the students' pre-employment training before they join RMN ships. It can also be included as a laboratory activity in the navigation science course. The lecturer must conduct briefings, training, and modules as part of the MLM implementation process.

2.4 Conclusion

All six attributes that contribute to the development of leadership among maritime operation students are OOW, critical thinking, decision-making, teamwork, communication skill, command, and control. To support this leadership framework, the students need to undergo the MLM using a ship navigation simulator. The methodology used for MLM in a simulator has proven to be highly effective in developing leaderships for the naval cadets of RMN. The lecturers play a crucial role as facilitators in ensuring the successful implementation of MLM for maritime operation students [10]. It is imperative that all students achieve these leadership attributes before graduating from their academic program. Successful graduates will be awarded with certificate of competency, which instills confidence in maritime agencies and the industry regarding their readiness to join these organizations.

References

1. Malaysia Ministry of Higher Education: Malaysia Education Blueprint 2015–2025 (Higher Education). Putrajaya: Malaysia MoHE (2015). https://jpt.mohe.gov.my/portal/index.php/en/corporate/policy-documents/16-malaysia-education-development-plan-2015-2025
2. E.S. Pudjiantoro, F.L. Pakpahan, H. Efendy, The transformation of leadership style in shaping the character of world class navy officer. Int. J. Hum. Resour. Stud. **7**(4), 72, 201 (2017). https://doi.org/10.5296/ijhrs.v7i4.11712
3. R.K. Branson, G.T. Rayner, J.L. Cox, J.P. Furman, F.J. King, W.H. Hannum, *Interservice Procedures for Instructional Systems Development: Executive Summary and Model*, vols. 1–5. TRADOC Pam 350–30, Ft. Monroe, VA: U.S. Army Training and Doctrine Command (1975)
4. Malaysia Ministry of Defence: Defence White Paper, Kuala Lumpur: Malaysia MoD (2019). https://www.mod.gov.my/images/mindef/article/kpp/DWP-3rd-Edition-02112020.pdf
5. P. Boissier, *Understanding a Nautical Chart: A Practical Guide to Safe Navigation*. (Fernhurst Books Limited, 2018)
6. G. Bosnick, *Tailored Approaches to Self-Leadership: A Bite-Size Approach Using Psychology and Neuroscience*. (Routledge, 2022)
7. M.R. Zulkifly, T.J. Weng, H.M. Eusoff, S. Isnan, A. Aziz, Creation of ship navigation data using simulation technology in training module. Trans. Marit. Sci. **10**(2), 355–360 (2021). https://doi.org/10.7225/toms.v10.n02.w03

8. Y. Lian, H. Duan, X. Yu, Advances in Guidance, Navigation and Control: Proceedings of 2020 International Conference on Guidance, Navigation and Control, ICGNC 2020, Tianjin, China, October 23–25, 2020. (Springer Nature, 2021)
9. J.W. Greswell, J.D. Greswell, *Research Design Qualitative, Quantitative and Mixed Method*, 5th edn. (Sage Publication, USA, 2018)
10. J.L. Barnhart, Elite and True: Leadership Lessons Inspired by the US Navy. (Greenleaf Book Group Press, 2022)

Chapter 3
Assessing the Efficiency of Cargo Distribution Using Road Freight Through Data Envelopment Analysis

Nik Norfara Idayu Mohd Zain, Kasypi Mokhtar, Wan Muhamad Amir Wan Ahmad, Siti Marsila Muhd Ruslan, and Roslin Ramli

Abstract The cargo distribution of road freight efficiency balances the trade-off between economic and environmental benefits. Increased road freight efficiency boosts economic growth, employment and work. Factors include population growth, urbanisation, globalisation, digitalisation and demographic demand for future freight transport to improve distribution system services. However, transportation research has been focused on passenger transport but lacks on goods transport. Thus, this study aims to evaluate the efficiency and productivity levels of road freight distribution in the Peninsular Malaysia. Data Envelopment Analysis, CCR and BCC model were used to assess the 11-year efficiency and productivity from 2005 to 2015. Findings implied that multiple factors influence the efficiency levels of road freight cargo distribution, such as geographical terrains, tourism, road expansion, transportation centralisation, urbanisation, economy, weather, road conditions and synergistic interactions of factors.

N. N. I. M. Zain (✉) · R. Ramli
Malaysian Institute of Marine Engineering Technology, Universiti Kuala Lumpur, Dataran Industri Teknologi Kejuruteraan Marin, Bandar Teknologi Maritim, Lumut, Perak, Malaysia
e-mail: norfara@unikl.edu.my

R. Ramli
e-mail: roslin@unikl.edu.my

N. N. I. M. Zain · K. Mokhtar · S. M. M. Ruslan
Faculty of Maritime Studies, Universiti Malaysia Terengganu, Kuala Nerus, Terengganu, Malaysia
e-mail: kasypi@umt.edu.my

S. M. M. Ruslan
e-mail: s.marsila@umt.edu.my

W. M. A. W. Ahmad
Department of Biostatistics, School of Dental Sciences, Universiti Sains Malaysia, Kota Bharu, Kelantan, Malaysia
e-mail: wmamir@usm.my

A. Ismail et al. (eds.), *Emerging Technologies and Sustainable Solutions*, SpringerBriefs in Applied Sciences and Technology,
https://doi.org/10.1007/978-3-032-18181-7_3

Keywords DEA · Efficiency · Road freight · BCC · CCR

3.1 Introduction

The booming progress of e-commerce became one of the major contributions to the current economic growth not only in Malaysia but also worldwide. E-commerce generates huge demands for freight volume and has given a massive boost to cargo traffic [1]. As a result, now the cargo logistics providers need to adapt to meet this new demand by providing the best service to the customers. The logistics system has also been facing development in order to accommodate these new changes because the performance of freight movement is crucial for the smooth operation of the whole logistics system. Therefore, determining the efficiency of the freight movement might pose a motivation that can enhance industry performance, particularly for road freight movement since transport infrastructure in most countries is dominated by road networks [2].

Road freight is practically one of the logistics services that we need to have to have an easier everyday life. The term 'freight' sums up a variety of movements, including freight couriers, consumers moving goods, waste management services, bulk materials transport and commercial vehicles [3]. In other words, road freight is also known as a system that frequently uses power-driven machinery to transport people, raw materials and merchandise both domestically and internationally [4]. This paper aims to evaluate the efficiency level of road freight distribution in the Peninsular Malaysia using data envelopment analysis (DEA), Charnes, Cooper and Rhodes (CCR) and Banker, Charnes and Cooper (BCC) analysis.

3.2 Methodology

The DEA was established in 1978 by Charnes, Cooper and Rhodes. A single measure of efficiency using linear programming is provided by the DEA linear programming technique [5]. A piece-wise frontier 'enveloping' all possible input–output combinations (production possibility set) for each decision-making unit (DMU) is used in the formulation of DEA, a non-parametric research methodology being used to assess the performance of a group of homogeneous decision-making units (DMUs). In relation to this study, the 12 states in the Peninsular Malaysia represented the different DMUs. Based on [6], the CCR DEA model can be described as follows: let us assume that there are n DMUs to be evaluated. Each DMU consumes m different inputs and produces s different outputs. Thus, DMU_j consumes X_{ij} of input i and produces Y_{rj} of output r. We also assume that $X_{\text{ij}} \geq 0$, $Y_{\text{rj}} \geq 0$ and for each DMU, so that there is one positive input and one positive output. From these, the ratio of outputs to inputs is used to measure relative efficiency $\text{DMU}_\text{j} = \text{DMU}_0$, the DMU to be evaluated relative to the ratio of all $j = 1, 2, \ldots, n$ DMU_{js}.

Therefore, for the current research, duty imports that represent revenue are the examples of output, whereas the number of goods vehicles, the length of federal roads and the length of state roads are the examples of inputs. The CCR model's purpose is to evaluate the efficiency of a DMU (states in Peninsular Malaysia) relative to the best-observed practice in a sample of n DMUs (n = 1, 2, …, N), where each one of them utilises a vector of i inputs (i = 1, 2, …, I) in order to produce a vector of m outputs (m = 1, 2, …, M), which are the dimensions of the inputs and outputs vectors that are ($I \times 1$) and ($M \times 1$), respectively. Strong disposability of inputs and outputs, the convexity of the set of practical input–output combinations, and CRS are three limitations imposed by the CCR model on emerging technologies [7]. This CCR model makes the assumption that a production process' inputs and outputs are unaffected by an operation's scale. The CRS model calculates each DMU's technical efficiency. The possibility production set P for CCR is:

$$\{(x, y)x \geq \lambda X, y \leq \lambda Y, \lambda \geq 0\} \tag{3.1}$$

The following linear programming models are the conventional CCR models for efficiency analysis. The CCR output-oriented Primal model are as below:

$$\text{Min } h_0 = \sum_{i=1}^{m} v_i x_{i0} \tag{3.2}$$

$$\sum_{i=1}^{m} v_i x_{ij} - \sum_{r=1}^{s} u_r y_{rj} \geq 0 j = 1, 2 \ldots\ldots.n$$

$$\sum_{r=1}^{s} u_r y_{r0} = 1$$

$$v_i, u_r 0\ i = 1, 2 \ldots\ldots m : r = 1, 2, \ldots s$$

The weighted outputs are set to unity and the weighted inputs are minimised in the output-oriented CCR primal model (2). The output weights u_r and inputs v_i are adjusted accordingly to generate an efficiency score which is given by $e_o = 1/h_o$. While the CCR primal model can generate both an efficiency score and the optimal output weights u_r and input weights v_i, the CCR dual model can be used to generate not only the efficiency score but also the composite inputs and outputs that the observed DMU_O should benchmark against λ_j is the reference weight for DMU_j (j = 1, 2, …, n) and $\lambda_j > 0$ means that DMU_j is used to construct the composite unit for DMU_O.

Note that the below models are based on CRS. This, however, disregards economies of scale. The output-oriented CCR dual model is given as follows:

$$\text{Max } h_0 = \theta_0 \tag{3.3}$$

Subject to

$$\sum_{j=1}^{n} \lambda_j y_{rj} \geq \theta_0 y_{r0} \; r = 1, 2, \ldots, s.$$

$$\sum_{j=1}^{n} \lambda_j x_{ij} \leq x_{i0} \quad i = 1, 2, \ldots, m.$$

$$\lambda_j \geq 0 \quad j = 1, 2, \ldots\ldots, n$$

By embracing the VRS assumption, which either increase or decreases CRS, [8] attempted to extend and further elaborate the basic CCR model by developing the BCC model. According to [5], the definition of the BCC possibility production set P is as follows:

$$P = \left\{ (x, y)x \geq \lambda X, y \leq \lambda Y \sum_{n-1}^{N} \lambda_n = 1 \; \lambda \geq 0 \right\} \tag{3.4}$$

The BCC model was suggested by [7] which relaxes the assumption of CRS and imposes VRS by adding the constraint $\sum_{n=1}^{N} \lambda_n = 1$. This addition is a crucial intervention because, if all input and output weights add up to 1, then efficiency factors for comparing various DMUs are convex combinations of actual observations. The equation for the BCC model output oriented is shown below. For this equation, a study by [8] involved adding an additional constant variable in order to permit VRS.

$$\text{Max Z} = \sum_{r=1}^{s} u_r y_{ro} - u_o \tag{3.5}$$

Subject to

$$\sum_{r=1}^{s} u_r y_{rj} - \sum_{i=1}^{m} v_i x_{ij} - u_o \leq 0 \quad j = 1, 2, \ldots, n$$

$$\sum_{i=1}^{m} v_i x_{io} = 1 \quad v_i \geq \varepsilon, u_r \geq$$

Basic information on whether a firm may enhance its performance in relation to the group of enterprises to which it is being compared is generated from the two DEA models mentioned above, namely the CCR model and the BCC model. Because the production frontier may move, various firms are likely to produce different efficiency results.

3.3 Results and Discussion

The output and input for this study were collected from 12 the states in the Peninsular Malaysia for the duration of 11 years from 2005 until 2015. The output is the value of duty import as a representative of revenue, while the input is the number of goods vehicles, the length or distance of the federal roads (km) and the length or distance of state roads (km).

A typical DEA model compares the effectiveness of related components based on pre-set inputs and outputs. A score of one indicates an efficient unit because efficiency is defined as the ratio of the weighted sum of outputs to the weighted sum of inputs [8]. In output-oriented models, the goal is to maximise outputs using the fewest possible inputs, as opposed to input-oriented models, where the goal is to maintain the same outputs with the fewest possible inputs [9]. The findings are defined in such a way that the DMU is thought to be fully efficient if theta = 1. However, it is considered inefficient if theta is less than 1 [10]. Hence, if the value is less than 1, the inputs are not being used appropriately and are being squandered to some extent for a variety of reasons [11].

Table 3.1 presents the top ten ranking of efficient DMUs based on the efficiency score result for CCRO analysis. According to Table 3.1, only four DMUs which are Perlis (2005), Selangor (2005), WPKL (2005) and WPKL (2007) showed the result of 1, which represents full efficiency level, within the time frame from 2005 to 2015. Based on this table, WPKL was the most leading DMU among the 12 states in the Peninsular Malaysia, followed by Perlis, Selangor and Penang.

The relative effectiveness and ranking of the efficiency of a resource's use are measured by DEA analysis, which examines a resource's total input and output [12].

The BCC model differs from the CCR model by scale assumptions. This is because the BCC model measures technical efficiency with the convexity constraint, which admits VRS. Table 3.2 describes the ranking of the DMU based on the BCCO analysis. Based on this table, only four states achieved the top ten efficiency ranking.

Table 3.1 Ranking of DMU for CCRO

DMU	Efficiency score	Rank
PERLIS2005	1	1
SLGR2005	1	1
WPKL2005	1	1
WPKL2007	1	1
WPKL2006	0.90594	5
WPKL2014	0.83674	6
PENANG2007	0.7599	7
WPKL2015	0.74331	8
WPKL2010	0.72326	9
PERLIS2006	0.72308	10

Table 3.2 Ranking of DMU for BCCO

DMU	Efficiency score	Rank
PERLIS2005	1	1
SLGR2005	1	1
WPKL2005	1	1
PERLIS2007	1	1
WPKL2007	1	1
WPKL2014	1	1
PENANG2007	0.96603	7
PENANG2006	0.93836	8
WPKL2015	0.91157	9
WPKL2006	0.90594	10

They were Perlis, Selangor, WPKL and Penang. Results implied that four states were efficient, the states were as follows: Perlis (2005), Selangor (2005), Perlis (2007), as well as WPKL in 2005, 2007 and 2014.

In this section, the efficiency level of the road freight cargo distribution in the Peninsular Malaysia measured by the DEA method using CCR and BCC analyses was discussed. The efficiency levels for each state in the Peninsular Malaysia were examined each year from 2005 until 2015. Efficiency refers to how effectively resources are utilised. Therefore, when the outputs are fixed, efficiency refers to either the maximisation of the outputs or minimisation of the inputs. Each state in the Peninsular Malaysia is very diverse in size. Hence, the data for length of roads, either federal roads or state roads, also differ in range. In the Peninsular Malaysia, only four states have container ports, which are Johor, Pahang, Selangor and Penang. Therefore, the revenues for these four states are very high compared to the other eight states. The number of goods vehicles also play a big role that contributed to the discrepancy of the efficiency scores.

The CCRO results showed that only three states, Perlis (2005), Selangor (2005) WPKL (2005 and 2007) reached efficiency, indicating that in the Peninsular Malaysia only these three states utilised their resources efficiently. Similar studies related to the efficiency of road freight have also been carried out recently. The most closely related recent study was carried out by [13] in the year 2019. According to [13], the analysis demonstrated that increasing investments in urban development and road transportation were insufficient to guarantee sustainable urban growth. To achieve local, regional and national development goals, policy must instead encourage the full utilisation of available resources in accordance with local conditions [13].

Authors of [14] also analysed the road freight efficiency in Europe from 2000 to 2012 but used the stochastic frontier analysis for the road efficiency model. According to [14], the goal of policy should be to maintain high efficiency. Due to the higher infrastructure needs and reduced efficiency caused by a relatively lower population density, some nations may be willing to accept a lower level of efficiency [14]. The results of the current investigation confirm the idea that a variety of factors influence the efficiency levels of road freight [13].

According to [13], because of the restrictions imposed by the steep and hilly terrains, the distribution and development of the built-up area in the Hunan province are unequal. In the present study, several rural states namely Terengganu, Kelantan and Pahang, are also geographically restricted by mountainous and high terrains. Authors of [13] reported that flat regions in their study area showed relatively concentrated built-up areas, which has also been observed in WPKL and Selangor in the present study. Furthermore, [13] also mentioned that Zhangjiajie is the city with the highest tourism resources, causing a drive in GDP growth and thus high efficiency. In comparison to the present study, highly urbanised areas such as Selangor and WPKL also possess a high tourism economy, which likely further contributes to road expansion and thus higher efficiency scores. However, the uneven distribution of built-up regions will enhance disparity and imbalance in development levels across different locations because of the rapid expansion of road transportation inside metropolitan areas, having unforeseeable implications [13].

The aforementioned elements—terrain and tourism—in turn, encouraged Changsha's level of urbanisation to be significantly higher than that of the other cities in Hunan province, propelling Changsha's growth into the nation's primary transportation centre [13]. For Peninsular Malaysia, Selangor is considered the central transportation hub partially contributed by its proximity to the metropolis and the presence of two international ports in Klang known as Port Klang, also known as North Port and West Port.

Subsequently, topographical limits impact the costs and rate of city and road expansion, resulting in inadequate urbanisation and road infrastructure, which could ultimately cause Shaoyang's economy to lag behind neighbouring Hunan cities and result in its low efficiency [13]. Similarly, the higher presence of urbanisation and urban population in Malaysian states also affects the efficiency level [15]. The findings of the present study also revealed that the top four efficiency ranking through CCR and BCC by states were WPKL, Selangor, Perlis and Penang. The road freight efficiency of states corresponds with the urban population of states, which ranked from the highest estimated urban population in the order of WPKL (100%), Selangor (90%) and Penang (90%). Perlis was considered to have a low urban population but high efficiency due to its geography in the same case as the study by [13].

3.4 Conclusion

Regarding other aspects of the distribution of road-borne freight, this analysis has some shortcomings. Since the primary objective of this study is to ascertain the level of efficiency of the road freight cargo distribution in the Peninsular Malaysia, other factors, such as environmental, policy and economic considerations are not considered because this paper focuses primarily on the operation aspect of the road cargo distribution. However, the study can be expanded by incorporating a wider geographical range, such as East Malaysia, and integrating qualitative analysis models in multicriteria decision-making. Therefore, future research should look more closely at several factors that affect how efficiently cargo is distributed, including employability, green logistics and other factors. However, this study can still serve as a guide for the next performance evaluations not only in the Peninsular Malaysia but also for all of Malaysia and other nations.

References

1. T. Bosona, Urban freight last mile logistics—challenges and opportunities to improve sustainability: a literature review. Sustainability (Switzerland) **12**(21), 1–20 (2020). https://doi.org/10.3390/su12218769
2. S. Gibbons, T. Lyytikäinen, H.G. Overman, R. Sanchis-Guarner, New Road infrastructure: the effects on firms. J. Urban Econ. **110**, 35–50 (2019). https://doi.org/10.1016/J.JUE.2019.01.002
3. R.B. Ellison, C. Teye, D.A. Hensher, Modelling sydney's light commercial service vehicles. Transp. Res. Part A Policy Pract. **96**, 79–89 (2017). https://doi.org/10.1016/J.TRA.2016.12.002
4. G. Wilson, J.M. Felix (2015) Transportation and National Development, Online (2015). Available: www.iiste.org
5. E. Thanassoulis, M.C.A. Silva, Measuring efficiency through data envelopment analysis. Impact **218**(1), 37–41 (2018). https://doi.org/10.1080/2058802x.2018.1440814
6. W.W. Cooper, H. Deng, Z. Huang, S.X. Li, Chance constrained programming approaches to congestion in stochastic data envelopment analysis. Eur. J. Oper. Res. **155**(2), 487–501 (2004). https://doi.org/10.1016/S0377-2217(02)00901-3
7. L.R. Murillo-Zamorano, Economic Efficiency and Frontier Techniques (2004)
8. R.D. Banker, A. Charnes, W.W. Cooper, Some models for estimating technical and scale inefficiencies in data envelopment analysis. Manage. Sci. **30**(9), 1078–1092 (1984)
9. G. Fancello, M. Carta, P. Serra, Data envelopment analysis for the assessment of road safety in urban road networks: a comparative study using CCR and BCC models. Case Stud. Transp. Policy **8**(3), 736–744 (2020). https://doi.org/10.1016/J.CSTP.2020.07.007
10. A. Charnes, W.W. Cooper, E. Rhodes, Measuring the efficiency of decision-making units. Eur. J. Oper. Res. **2**(6), 429–444 (1978). https://doi.org/10.1016/0377-2217(78)90138-8
11. F.S. Mustafa, R.U. Khan, T. Mustafa, Technical efficiency comparison of container ports in Asian and Middle East region using DEA. Asian J. Shipping Logistics **37**(1), 12–19 (2021). https://doi.org/10.1016/J.AJSL.2020.04.004
12. Z. Pan, Y. Wang, Y. Zhou, Y. Wang, Analysis of the water use efficiency using super-efficiency data envelopment analysis. Appl. Water Sci. **10**(6), (2020). https://doi.org/10.1007/s13201-020-01223-1
13. T. Yang, X. Guan, Y. Qian, W. Xing, H. Wu (2019) Efficiency evaluation of urban road transport and land use in Hunan Province of China based on hybrid data envelopment analysis (DEA) models. Sustain. (Switz.) **11**(14). https://doi.org/10.3390/su11143826
14. B. Wiegmans, A. Champagne-Gelinas, S. Duchesne, B. Slack, P. Witte, Rail and road freight transport network efficiency of Canada, member states of the EU, and the USA. Res. Transp. Bus. Manag. **28**, 54–65 (2018). https://doi.org/10.1016/J.RTBM.2018.10.004
15. K.P. Tan, K.D. Kanniah, A.P. Cracknell, On the upstream inputs into the MODIS primary productivity products using biometric data from oil palm plantations. Int. J. Remote Sens. **35**(6), 2215–2246 (2014). https://doi.org/10.1080/01431161.2014.889865

Chapter 4
Factors that Influence the Sustainability of Insurance Companies in Malaysia in Facing the Issue of Phase Liberalization

Mohd Sharifuddin Ahmad, Ahmad Faizal Ahmad Fuad, Mohd Saiful Izwaan Saadon, Norlinda Mohd Rozar, and Loke Keng Bin

Abstract The initial phase of liberalization of motor and fire tariffs, enacted on July 1, 2016, aimed to evaluate its impact on insurance companies and policyholders. This initiative granted insurers operators the freedom to introduce new products and expand coverage at competitive market rates. This liberalization enabled insurers to tailor premiums based on individual needs, fostering intense competition and sustainability. Larger companies with substantial capital could dominate the market by absorbing slim profit margins. The research aimed to enhance insurance company competitiveness amidst this liberalization in Malaysia by identifying influential factors and subfactors and prioritizing them. Financial strength and solvency emerged as the most significant factor, outweighing others such as product service innovation, market segmentation and targeting, operational efficiency, cost optimization and customer service and engagement.

Keywords Phase liberalization · Financial strength and solvency · Product service innovation · Market segmentation and targeting · Operational efficiency and cost optimization

---

M. S. Ahmad · A. F. A. Fuad (✉) · M. S. I. Saadon · N. M. Rozar · L. K. Bin
Faculty of Maritime Studies, Universiti Malaysia Terengganu, Kuala Terengganu, Terengganu, Malaysia
e-mail: faizalfuad75@gmail.com

M. S. Ahmad
e-mail: mohdsharifuddin@umt.edu.my

M. S. I. Saadon
e-mail: saiful.izwan@umt.edu.my

N. M. Rozar
e-mail: norlinda.rozar@umt.edu.my

L. K. Bin
e-mail: loke.k@umt.edu.my

A. Ismail et al. (eds.), *Emerging Technologies and Sustainable Solutions*, SpringerBriefs in Applied Sciences and Technology,
https://doi.org/10.1007/978-3-032-18181-7_4

4.1 Introduction

The liberalization of motor and fire tariffs, initiated in July 2016, aimed to gauge its effects on insurers and policyholders by granting them flexibility to introduce new products and expand coverage at market rates. This flexibility extended to third-party fire and theft products in 2017 [1]. Premiums now reflect comprehensive risk assessment, allowing insurers to tailor pricing to individual needs. Consequently, consumers gravitate towards companies offering optimal risk protection at minimal premiums, benefiting larger firms capable of withstanding slim profit margins [2]. This fosters intense competitiveness, favouring companies with substantial capital to maintain profitability. Research seeks to bolster insurers' competitiveness amidst liberalization's impact in Malaysia. Objectives include identifying factors influencing competitiveness and devising a hierarchical framework to prioritize these factors for insurers.

Insurance companies face challenges in economic, political and legal spheres, necessitating innovation in products and services for competitiveness. Effective innovation enhances sustainability and attracts customers [3]. Continuous development of products and services is crucial to meet consumer demands and ensure company viability, as obsolete offerings have diminishing demand [4]. Service-oriented value addition is paramount for competitiveness, particularly in a saturated market [5]. Incorporating technology to innovate risk assessment processes enhances efficiency and reduces errors and delays [6]. For instance, blockchain technology can streamline insurance activities, increase premium accuracy and minimize costs. Product and service innovation, encompassing unique offerings, value-added services and technological integration, is pivotal for competitiveness amidst liberalization.

Market segmentation and targeting are crucial factors for insurance companies. By identifying potential customers and tailoring products and services to meet their specific needs, competitive companies can ensure long-term survival [7]. Offering segment-oriented solutions aligned with regulatory changes and market dynamics is essential for success. Effective marketing strategies that resonate with targeted customer segments enhance credibility and drive subscriptions [8]. Segment-specific problem-solving approaches further strengthen a company's competitive position. In essence, market segmentation, coupled with problem-solving initiatives, forms a potent marketing strategy essential for long-term sustainability in the insurance industry [9].

4.2 Methodology

The research applied analytic hierarchy process (AHP) to organize and analyse the factors and subfactors hierarchically. The flowchart of the research activities is shown in Fig. 4.1.

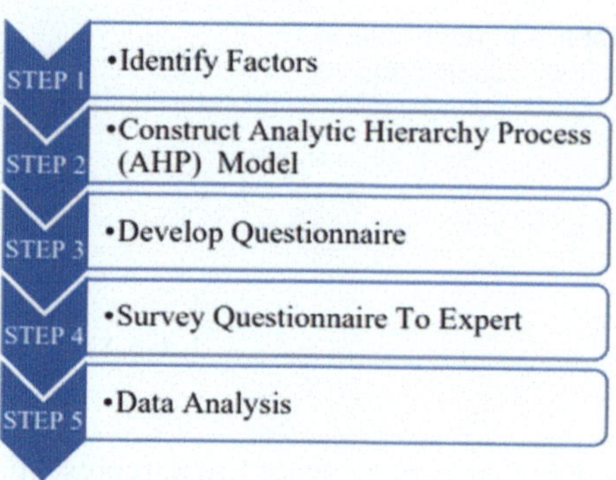

Fig. 4.1 Flowchart of research activities

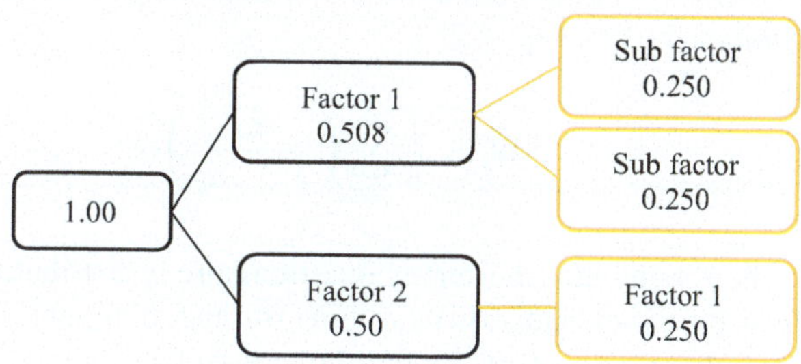

Fig. 4.2 AHP model

The research started by identifying the factors and subfactors that influence company effectiveness. This was conducted through a literature review on various resources such as books, journals, proceedings and any related material. The systematic review to identify the related factors and subfactors is concluded before the AHP method is applied.

The next step is to develop a factor hierarchical model for ranking purposes (AHP). The data from the literature review is used to construct the AHP model, which is shown in Fig. 4.2. It's comprising of three levels, i.e. goal, factors and subfactors.

The third stage involves creating a questionnaire through the utilization of the pair-wise comparison technique. This approach is employed to determine the relative weight of each factor. The pair-wise comparison technique entails arranging the n factors in both the rows and columns of a $n \times n$ matrix. Subsequently, a ratio scale is applied to the matrix, as illustrated in Table 4.1.

The certified judgement on pairs of attributes A_i and A_j are represented by a $n \times n$ a matrix A as shown in Eq. (4.1).

$$A = (a_{ij}) = \begin{bmatrix} 1 & a_{12} & \ldots a_{1n} \\ a/a_{12} & 1 & \ldots a_{2n} \\ 1/a_{1n} & 1/a_{2n} & \ldots 1 \end{bmatrix} \tag{4.1}$$

Table 4.1 Ratio scale of pair-wise comparison

Numerical assessment	Linguistic meaning
1	Equal importance
3	Moderate importance
5	Strong Importance
7	Very importance
9	Extremely importance
2, 4, 6, 8	Intermediate values of important

where i and j range from 1 to n, representing attributes A_i and A_j, respectively. Each a_{ij} denotes the relative importance of attribute A_i to attribute A_j. For a matrix of order n, (n x (n − 1)/2) comparisons are necessary. The weight value of each factor is computed using Eq. (4.2).

$$W_k = \frac{1}{n}\sum_{j=1}^{n}\left(\frac{a_{kj}}{\sum_{i=1}^{n} a_{ij}}\right)(k = 1, 2, 3, \ldots, n) \tag{4.2}$$

Following this, the survey questionnaire is distributed to experts, who are chosen from prominent individuals within insurance companies. Subsequently, the data analysis phase involves assessing the consistency ratio (*CR*) derived from the weight values obtained in the pair-wise comparison matrix. The *CR* value is computed utilizing specific equations.

$$CR = \frac{CI}{R1}$$

$$CI = \frac{\lambda_{\max - n}}{n - 1}$$

$$\lambda_{\max} = \frac{\sum_{j=1}^{n} \frac{\sum_{k=1}^{n} w_k a\, jk}{w_j}}{n} \tag{4.3}$$

Within this framework, 'n' signifies the number of items being compared, with 'λmax' denoting the maximum weight value found within the comparison matrix of dimensions $n \times n$. '*RI*' stands for random index, and '*CI*' denotes the consistency index. Table 4.2 provides the random index values. A *CR* value exceeding 0.10 signifies inconsistency in pair-wise comparisons, whereas a *CR* of 0.10 or lower indicates a reasonable level of consistency in the pair-wise comparisons.

Table 4.2 Table of random index

N	1	2	3	4	5	6	7	8	9	10	11	12	13
RI	0	0	0.58	0.90	1.12	1.24	1.32	1.41	1.45	1.49	1.51	1.58	1.56

4.3 Result and Discussion

The results of the submission of questionnaires and explanations from experts found that the factors and subfactors of the study are in line with the current situation and needs of insurance companies. Factors and subfactors give a real picture of the steps that need to be taken by the insurance side to be competitive and sustainable. The factors and subfactors that have been constructed are as stated in Table 4.3.

4.3.1 Weight Stage Main Factors

Figure 4.3 shows the weight of main factors that influence the efficiency of insurance company. The financial strength and solvency are the highest main factors that weight 47.47% indicates that the insurance company must enhance on financial stability, prudent investment and transparent reporting in order to become a sustainable company. The second rank is product and service innovation to attract

Table 4.3 Factors and subfactors

Main factors	Products and service innovation:	Rajapathirana and Hui [3]
Sub 1	Innovative products	Mgeryan et al. [4]
Sub 2	Value-added services	Wang et al. [5]
Sub 3	Technology adoption	Lanfranchi and Grassi [6]
Main factors	Market segmentation and targeting:	Qadadeh and Abdallah [7]
Sub 1	Segment identification and solution	Schreiber [8]
Sub 2	Effective marketing	Abdul Rahman et al. [9]
Main factors	Operational efficiency and cost optimization	Wongchai (2017) Chmieloweic-Lewczuk (2019)
Sub 1	Process streamlining	Mgeryan et al. [4] Almira Rhea Masayu (2018)
Sub 2	Digitalization and automation	M, L. (2020) O, O. S. (2021)
Sub 3	Risk management	Fursova (2021)
Main factors	Customer experience and engagement	Malani (2017) Woerner (2018)
Sub 1	Customer–centric approach	Imira Manafzadeh (2016) Mahieux (2016)
Sub 2	Feedback utilization	Christian Eckert (2022)
Main factors	Financial strength and solvency	Necas (2016)
Sub 1	Financial stability	Necas (2016)
Sub 2	Prudent investments	An Chen (2018)
Sub 3	Transparent reporting	Tomic (2022)

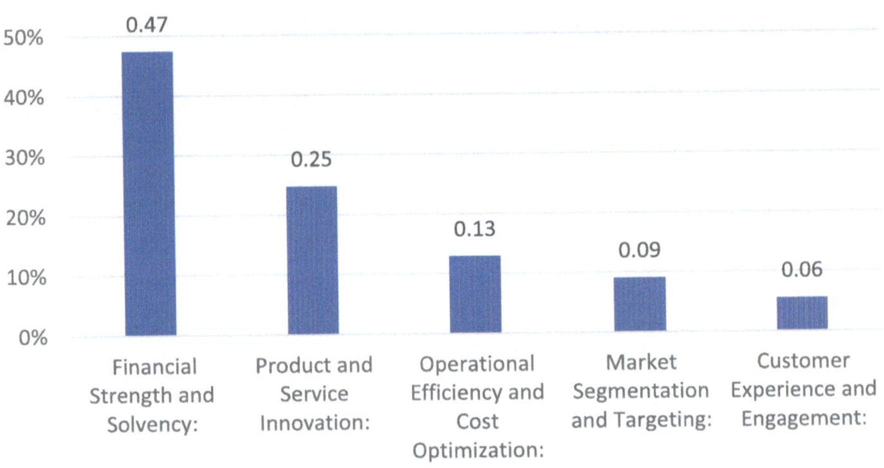

Fig. 4.3 Main factors weight

customer to engage with the business weight 24.80%. The adoption of technology, value added in the service is the second important to ensure the innovative product meet the demand of client. It follows by operational efficiency and cost optimization by 12.98%. The digitalization is the key factor that enhances the efficiency of the daily operational management of an insurance company. Market segmentation and targeting that weight 9.13% is the second last in weight. However, it is still as important as the others factors since the effective marketing is the heart of business. The lowest in rank is customer experience and engagement that weight 5.63%. It is due to the engagement of customer which is established by the product and time period of the insurance product. The engagement will establish via financial stability of the company to indemnify the loss.

4.3.2 Consolidated Result

Figure 4.4 displays the consolidated results of all subfactors under main factors. Financial stability holds the highest rank, weighing 29.78%, followed by innovative product development, prudent investment, digitalization, market segmentation, transparent reporting, value-added services, customer-centric approach, technology adoption, risk management, effective marketing, streamlined processes and feedback utilization. This underscores the crucial role of financial stability in ensuring the insurance company sustainability, as noted by experts, potentially positioning financially robust companies to dominate the market.

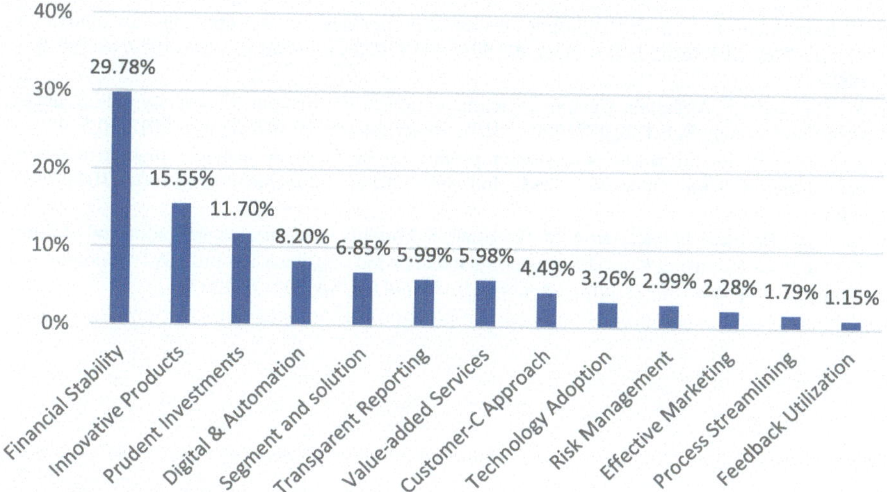

Fig. 4.4 Consolidates result

4.4 Conclusion

In summary, financial stability is the main factors to the sustainability of insurance companies. However, other factors also play an important role and affect the competitive power of the company. A successful company will take into account all the factors that improve the company's ability from financial aspects, products, services and also customers.

Acknowledgements The research team would like to thanks the Holistic Lab of University Technology Malaysia, which has partly financed this research.

References

1. Bank Negara Malaysia: Liberisation of Motor Insurance. https://www.bnm.gov.my/-/liberalisation-of-motor-insurance-1. (2017)
2. Mahpar, N.: Risko Perang Harga Insuran. https://www.bharian.com.my/taxonomy/term/5/2016/08/183478/risiko-perang-harga-industri-insurans. (2016)
3. R.P.J. Rajapathirana, Y. Hui, Relationship between innovation capability, innovation type, and firm performance. J. Innov. Knowl. **3**, 44–55 (2018). https://doi.org/10.1016/j.jik.2017.06.002
4. M. Mgeryan, G. Fedotova, V. Borulko, A. Kulakov, Y. Kapustina, Innovative opportunities for insurance development in a new financial paradigm. SHS Web Conf. **93**, 02016 (2021). https://doi.org/10.1051/shsconf/20219302016
5. Y. Wang, X. Rong, H. Zhao, D. Li, Optimal investment problem between two insurers with value-added service. Commun. Stat. Theory Methods. **50**, 1781–1806 (2019)

6. D. Lanfranchi, L. Grassi, Examining insurance companies use of technology for innovation. Geneva Pap. Risk Insur. Issues Pract. **47**, 520–537 (2022). https://doi.org/10.1057/s41288-021-00258-y
7. W. Qadadeh, S. Abdallah, Customers segmentation in the insurance company (TIC) dataset. Procedia Comput. Sci. **144**, 277–290 (2018). https://doi.org/10.1016/j.procs.2018.10.529
8. F. Schreiber, Identification of customer groups in the German term life market: a benefit segmentation. Ann. Oper. Res. **254**, 365–399 (2017). https://doi.org/10.1007/s10479-017-2446-y
9. S. Abdul-Rahman, N.F.K. Arifin, M. Hanafiah, S. Mutalib, Customer segmentation and profiling for life insurance using K-modes clustering and decision tree classifier. Int. J. Adv. Comput. Sci. Appl. **12**, 434–444 (2021). https://doi.org/10.14569/IJACSA.2021.0120950

Chapter 5
The Use of Multiple Linear Regression to Predict Inter-industry Knowledge Sharing: The Effect of Port Workers' Non-technological Determinants

Mohd Zarir Yusoff, Mohd Saiful Izwaan Saadon, Muhammad Ammar Shafi, Hafizah Zulkipli, and Fadillah Ismail

Abstract Researchers aim to examine the influence of non-technological determinants (personnel, colleagues, and organization) and port workers' intention to share their knowledge to other industries. The sample included seven major federal port operator companies, chosen using random sampling. A questionnaire was used to distribute to knowledge workers in Malaysia's port operator industry. The study found that personnel factors have a significant direct impact on the intention to share knowledge among workers in the port industries. The highest value of weightage was 0.3. This finding contributes to the existing understanding on the extent of personnel, colleagues, and organizational factors in contributing to inter-industry knowledge sharing among port operator workers. The findings contribute to the existing understanding of the factors that contribute to inter-industry knowledge sharing among port operators and contribute to port operations excellence.

Keywords Inter-industry · Knowledge sharing · Port operators' industry · Non-technological determinants

---

M. Z. Yusoff (✉) · M. A. Shafi · H. Zulkipli · F. Ismail
Faculty Technology Management and Business, Universiti Tun Hussein Onn Malaysia, Parit Raja, Johor, Malaysia
e-mail: zarir@uthm.edu.my

M. A. Shafi
e-mail: ammar@uthm.edu.my

H. Zulkipli
e-mail: hafizahz@uthm.edu.my

F. Ismail
e-mail: fadillah@uthm.edu.my

M. S. I. Saadon
Faculty of Maritime Studies, Univesiti Malaysia Terengganu, Kuala Terengganu, Terengganu, Malaysia
e-mail: saiful.izwaan@umt.edu.my

A. Ismail et al. (eds.), *Emerging Technologies and Sustainable Solutions*,
SpringerBriefs in Applied Sciences and Technology,
https://doi.org/10.1007/978-3-032-18181-7_5

5.1 Introduction

Knowledge sharing is crucial in today's knowledge-driven economy, driving innovation and enhancing organizational performance. With technology advancements, organizations recognize its strategic value [1]. Research has explored factors influencing knowledge sharing within and between organizations, but there is limited focus on understanding inter-industry knowledge sharing, especially for port operator workers. Rapid development that is faced by the port industry have led to requirement for them to share the knowledge across sector to the potential employee aware and equip with the future knowledge, skills, and attitude [2]. Such act is important upon ensuring port operation excellence and sustaining their competitive level [3]. Unfortunately, previous research showed the knowledge sharing across sector among port operators is still at a slow pace. Knowledge sharing interpreted the acts of sharing ideas, solutions, and best practices across different personnel, department, industries, and even industries [4]. This can involve collaboration between companies, organizations, and personnels in different fields, sharing of manual and procedures, attachment in other industry, involvement in communities of practices with the goal of leveraging each other's expertise and experience to drive innovation and growth [5]. Understanding inter-industry knowledge sharing requires considering non-technological determinants. While technological factors like information systems and digital platforms significantly influence knowledge sharing behaviors, their influence cannot be overlooked, as they also play a crucial role in shaping knowledge sharing behaviors.

Research has indicated that personnel characteristics significantly influence knowledge sharing within and between organizations. Author [6], who conducted research in Saudi Arabia reveals personnel factors and technology acceptance significantly influence the academic staffs' knowledge sharing, emphasizing the importance of considering personnel characteristics in inter-industry knowledge sharing. Furthermore, organizational factors have been recognized as a critical driver of knowledge sharing. Authors of [7] proposed the concept of a knowledge-creating company, emphasizing the role of organizational culture in promoting knowledge sharing and creation. Organizations that foster a supportive culture, which values collaboration and knowledge sharing, are more likely to facilitate inter-industry knowledge exchange among their port operator workers [8]. In addition to personnel and organizational factors, colleagues' factors or often mentioned as social networks have also been identified as influential determinants of knowledge sharing.

This study explores the non-technological factors' role on igniting the behavior of knowledge sharing among the employees of port operator, including personnel, colleague, and organizational factors [9]. While previous research has examined these factors in the scope of knowledge sharing within organizations, their role in influencing on knowledge sharing between industries remains relatively unexplored.

5.2 Methodology

The statistical method linear regression often used to control the value of a dependent variable by considering the value of an independent variable, commonly known as a forecasting strategy, and is widely used. The following are the assumptions underlying the multiple linear regression model [10]:

(i) The x's following a linear and additive pattern defined the population mean of y within the level of the respondent's population.
(ii) It was believed that the y observations were statistically independent.
(iii) For all values of x, the standard deviation of y within the x-strata remained constant.
(iv) Within the x-strata, the distribution of y was normal.

All of the assumptions of multiple linear regression must be fulfilled prior to analyzing the data. The study relied on constant variance, normality, and multicollinearity as its assumptions. It ensured a uniform variance of errors and normal data distribution through residual analysis. Multicollinearity testing was performed using the variation inflation factor (VIF), indicating significant multicollinearity issues. Multiple linear regression included multiple predictor variables. This is the multiple linear regression model:

$$Y = \beta_0 + \beta_1 X_1 + \beta_2 X_2 + \ldots + \beta_j X_j + \varepsilon \quad (5.1)$$

where Y is the vector of responses (dependent variable), Beta $\beta_0, \beta_1, \ldots, \beta_j$ are the constants (regression coefficients), $X_1, X_2, \ldots, X_j$ are the independent variables (predictors), and ε is the vector of independent normal random variables (error term).

In matrix terms, the following matrices are defined:

$$Y = X\beta + \varepsilon \quad (5.2)$$

where $Y = [Y_1, Y_2, \ldots, Y_\text{n}]$ is a vector of responses (dependent variable) with n observations, value of X is the matrix of parameters, where each row represents an observation and each column corresponds to a predictor variable, $\beta = [\beta_0, \beta_1, \ldots, \beta_j]$ is a vector of constants (regression coefficients), and $\varepsilon = [\varepsilon_0, \varepsilon_1, \ldots, \varepsilon_n]$ is a vector of independent normal random variables (error term).

The following are the variance analysis sums of squares in matrix terms:

$$\text{SSR} = bX'Y - (1/n)Y'JY \quad (5.3)$$

$$\text{SSE} = (Y - Xb)'(Y - Xb) \quad (5.4)$$

$$\text{SST} = Y^{\wedge\prime}Y - (1/n)Y'JY \quad (5.5)$$

Table 5.1 Collinearity diagnostics

Model	Tolerance	VIF	Sigma value
Personnel factors	0.746	1.341	0.690
Colleagues' factors	0.550	1.817	0.166
Organizational factors	0.627	1.596	0.

where SSR is the sum of squares due to regression, SSE is the sum of squares of error, SST is the total sum of squares, X' denotes the transpose of matrix X' Y' denotes the transpose of vector Y, and J is a matrix of ones with appropriate dimensions.

Furthermore, there were distinct degrees of freedom for the sum of squares. In particular, SSR's degrees of freedom were p-1, where p is the number of parameters or predictor variables. However, SSE was found to be correlated with n-p degrees of freedom, where n is the study's sample size. SST is associated with n-1 degrees of freedom, as is typical. Data analysis tools include the ANOVA, mean square regression (MSR), and mean square error (MSE). An example of a risk function is the mean squared error (MSE), which stands for the quadratic loss value. It computes the mean squared "errors," or variations between the implied value of the estimator and the actual number, frequently resulting from chance or information omission. Table 5.1 offers an overview of the ANOVA. The following are the equations to calculate the MSR and MSE values:

$$\mathrm{MSR} = \frac{\mathrm{SSR}}{p-1} \tag{5.6}$$

$$\mathrm{MSE} = \frac{\mathrm{SSE}}{n-p} \tag{5.7}$$

5.3 Results and Discussion

The Residuals Variance

With the aid of the SPSS program, the residual variance was calculated. To determine the residual variance condition, a scatter plot was employed. Based on the data shown in Fig. 5.1, it appeared that the dots were dispersed and lacked any patterns. This study's residual variance has been verified.

The Residual Normality Distributed

This study examined the normality assumption in multiple linear regression, using a Q-Q plot for inter-industry knowledge sharing as a dependent variable. The Q-Q plot displayed in Fig. 5.2 indicates that the data points follow a straight line, confirming the normality assumption. Therefore, the normality assumption for the multiple linear regression was satisfied.

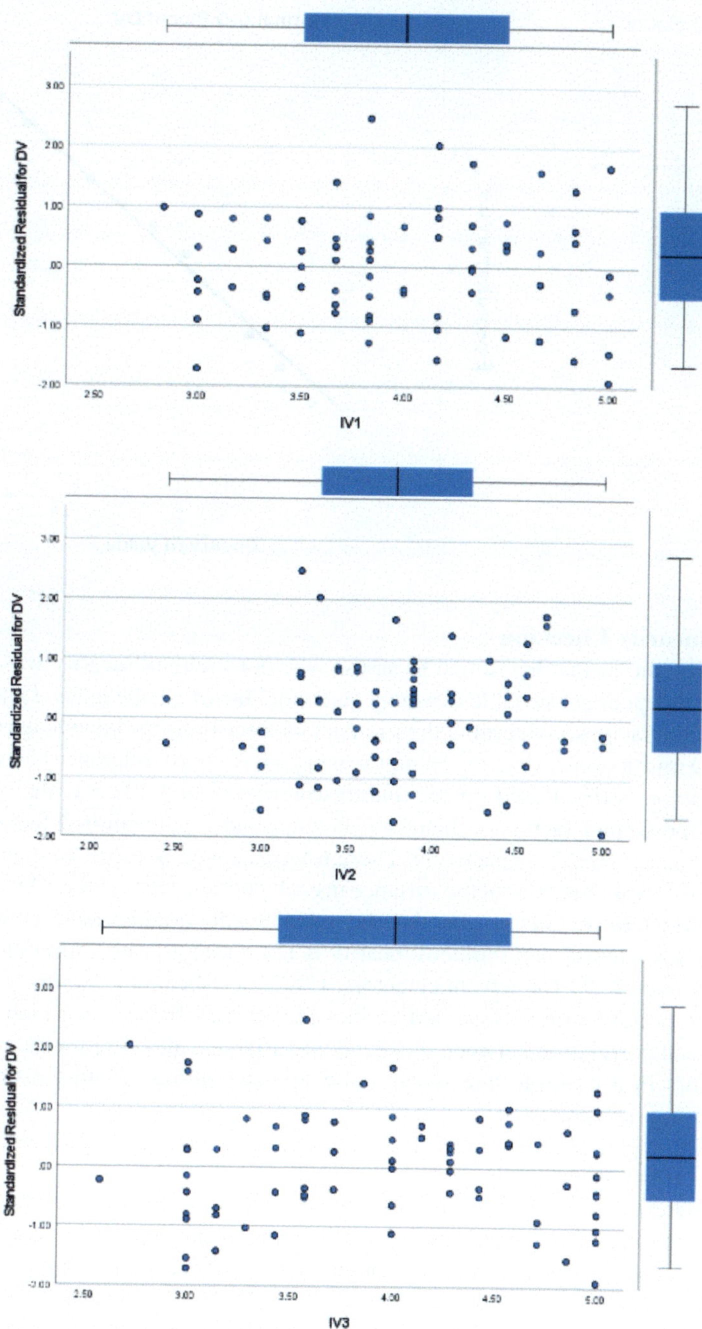

Fig. 5.1 Scatter plot of variance of residuals

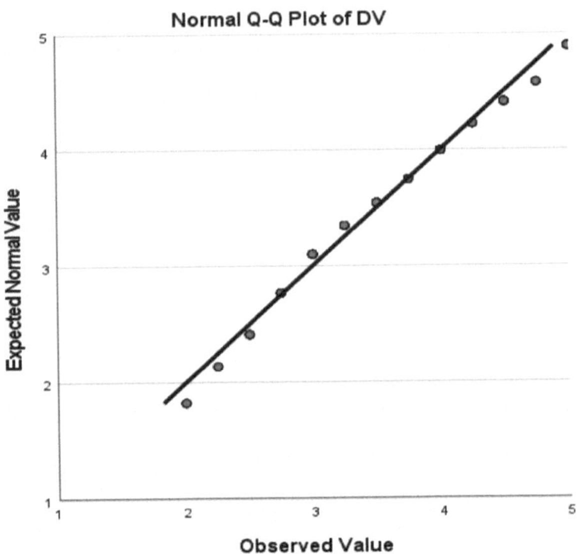

Fig. 5.2 Q-Q plot of normality

Multicollinearity Checking

In this study, the researcher aimed to assess whether multicollinearity was present among the independent variables, namely personnel factors, colleagues' factors, and organizational factors, concerning their impact on inter-industry knowledge sharing. To evaluate multicollinearity, two common metrics were used: tolerance and variance inflation factor (VIF). Based on the findings presented in Table 5.1, the tolerance values for personnel factors, colleagues' factors, and organizational factors were 0.746, 0.550, and 0.627, respectively. These tolerance values are all well above 0.5, indicating that less than 50% of the variance in each predictor is explained by the other variables. Thus, the results suggest that the independent variables have a reasonable level of independence, and multicollinearity is not a major issue. Additionally, the VIF values were 1.341 for personnel factors, 1.817 for colleagues' factors, and 1.596 for organizational factors. These VIF values are all well below 10, which indicate no significant correlation between independent variables, allowing for the inclusion of predictors in a multiple linear regression model without inflating estimates or compromising interpretation.

Multiple Linear Regression

The researchers used analysis of multiple linear regression to investigate the correlation between inter-industry knowledge sharing among port operators and three key factors: personnel factors, colleagues' factors, and organizational factors. The study reveals that personnel and colleague factors significantly influence inter-industry knowledge sharing among port operators, with a one-unit increase in either factor corresponding to a corresponding increase. This finding is aligned with the result from author [11]. Organizational factors' impact was not statistically significant, suggesting further investigation. The model provided a useful prediction equation for this relationship (Table 5.2). The equation is:

$$\hat{Y} = 0.926 + 0.300^{*}\text{Personnel factors} + 0.281^{*}\ \text{Colleague factors} \tag{5.8}$$

Analysis of Variance (ANOVA)

The ANOVA results show significant differences in the influence of personnel, colleagues', and organizational factors on inter-industry knowledge sharing among port operators. Based on the significant *F*-statistic of 25.163, which is smaller than the usual significance level of 0.05, and the corresponding *p*-value of 0.000, this conclusion is drawn. The multiple linear regression model is statistically significant, indicating that at least one independent variable significantly influences inter-industry knowledge sharing. The sum of mean squares is divided by the corresponding degrees of freedom to get the mean square. This average unexplained variability of the model's predictions is represented by the mean square residual, which comes in at 0.461. A smaller mean square residual indicates that the model's predictions are more accurate and precise. Port operators' inter-industry information sharing is highly influenced by organizational, coworker, and personnel characteristics, as revealed by the ANOVA results, which also support the relevance of the multiple linear regression model. The reliability of the model is indicated by a tiny mean square residual (Table 5.3).

Table 5.2 Multiple linear regression

Model		Unstandardized coefficients		Sig.
		B	Std. Error	
1	(Constant)	0.926	0.307	0.003
	Personnel factors	0.300	0.073	0.000
	Colleagues factors	0.281	0.094	0.003
	Organizational factors	0.094	0.069	0.177

*Significant at 0.05

Table 5.3 Analysis of variance or ANOVA

Model	Sum of squares	df	Mean square	*F*	Sig.
Regression	34.817	3	11.606	25.163	0.000
Residual	133.753	290	0.461		
Total	168.571	293			

5.4 Conclusion

This research article explores the factors driving inter-industry knowledge sharing among port operators, highlighting the importance of self-efficacy, image, and knowledge-efficacy. It also highlights the role of intrinsic motivation and knowledge sharing in fostering innovation and operational excellence in a collaborative culture. This study's limitations include its focus on the Malaysian port operator industry; its cross-sectional nature may hinder causal relationships. Longitudinal analysis could offer more dynamic insights. Despite these limitations, the study provides valuable insights for port industry stakeholders to optimize operations by fostering a culture of knowledge sharing. By addressing identified limitations and leveraging personnel and colleague factors, operators can drive continuous improvement and innovation.

Acknowledgements We would like to thank all the respondents from seven major federal ports in Malaysia who helped us to answer the questionnaires.

References

1. W. Tsai, S. Ghoshal, Social capital and value creation: the role of intrafirm networks. Acad. Manag. J. **41**(4), 464–476 (1998)
2. L. Ardito, R. Cerchione, E. Mazzola, E. Raguseo, Industry 4.0 transition: a systematic literature review combining the absorptive capacity theory and the data–information–knowledge hierarchy. J. Knowl. Manag. **26**(9), 2222–2254 (2022)
3. B. Kura, C. Dunn, A. Iyer, E.B. Ajdari, Promoting sustainability at the ports through knowledge sharing. J. Geosci. Environ. Protection. **2**(2), 143–150 (2014)
4. T.-M. Nguyen, Four-dimensional model: a literature review in online organizational knowledge sharing. VINE J. Inf. Knowl. Manag. Systems. **51**(1), 109–138 (2021)
5. M. Balde´, A.I. Ferreira, T. Maynard, Seci driven creativity: the role of team trust and intrinsic motivation. J. Knowl. Manag. **22**(8), 1688–1711 (2018)
6. D. Chandran, A.M. Alammari, Influence of culture on knowledge sharing attitude among academic staff in elearning virtual communities in Saudi Arabia. Inf. Syst. Front. **23**, 1563–1572 (2021)
7. I. Nonaka, H. Takeuchi, The knowledge-creating company: How Japanese companies create the dynamics of innovation. Long Range Plan. **29**(4), 592 (1996)
8. K.A. Al-Busaidi, L. Olfman, Knowledge sharing through inter-organizational knowledge sharing systems. VINE J. Inf. Knowl. Manag. Systems. **47**(1), 110–136 (2017)
9. M.T. Hansen, M.L. Mors, Løva°s, B., Knowledge sharing in organizations: Multiple networks, multiple phases. Acad. Manag. J. **48**(5), 776–793 (2005)
10. D.G. Pablo, A multiple linear regression analysis to measure the journal contribution to the social attention of research. Axioms MDPI, 1–15 (2023)
11. N. Mohammed, T. Kamalanabhan, Tacit knowledge seeking from teammates: unravelling the role of social capital. Int. J. Organ. Anal. **28**(3), 765–790 (2020)

Chapter 6
Blockchain Technologies in Cyber-physical Systems

Badlishah Ahmad, Naimah Yaakob, and Ong Bi Lynn

Abstract Cyber-physical systems (CPS) blend physical elements with integrated computing capabilities across interconnected networks, facilitating data exchange for various functionalities. However, CPS often suffer from drawbacks associated with centralized architectures, leading to vulnerabilities in security, reliability, and privacy. Inadequate data protection mechanisms can further exacerbate these issues. Blockchain technology offers a decentralized solution, employing sophisticated encryption for data transmission without relying on centralized intermediaries for verification and certification. Integration of CPS with blockchain shows promising features, enhancing security and resistance to tampering and fraud. This chapter explores various blockchain technologies applied in CPS, emphasizing their advantages and deployment across diverse applications. Additionally, it examines ongoing research efforts aimed at addressing security concerns within CPS environments.

Keywords Blockchain · Cyber-physical systems (CPS) · Security

6.1 Introduction

A cyber-physical system (CPS) integrates computation, communication, and physical processes to achieve specific goals or functions. This fusion of digital technology with the physical world enables the development of intelligent systems capable of sensing, acting, and adapting to their environment. CPS serves as the foundation for implementing Industry 4.0, exemplified by the deployment of smart

B. Ahmad · N. Yaakob · O. B. Lynn
Faculty of Intelligent Computing, Universiti Malaysia Perlis, Arau, Perlis, Malaysia
e-mail: naimahyaakob@unimap.edu.my

O. B. Lynn
e-mail: drlynn@unimap.edu.my

B. Ahmad (✉) · N. Yaakob · O. B. Lynn
Centre of Excellence for Advanced Computing, Universiti Malaysia Perlis, Arau, Perlis, Malaysia
e-mail: badli@unimap.edu.my

A. Ismail et al. (eds.), *Emerging Technologies and Sustainable Solutions*,
SpringerBriefs in Applied Sciences and Technology,
https://doi.org/10.1007/978-3-032-18181-7_6

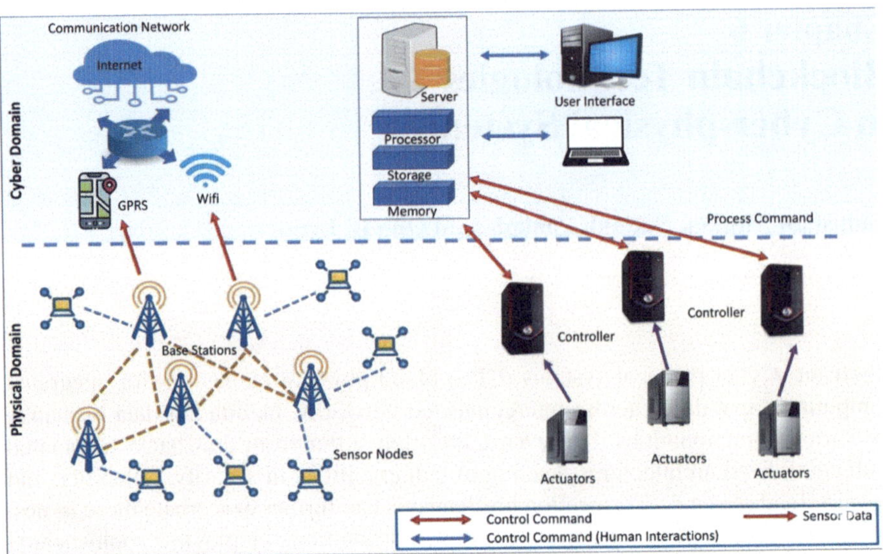

Fig. 6.1 CPS architecture

networked systems with embedded sensor nodes, controllers, and actuators. These components interact and communicate in real time, ensuring reliable performance in safety-critical applications, as illustrated in Fig. 6.1.

CPSs are found in various applications, including transportation, manufacturing, healthcare, and energy, to name just a few. CPSs have the potential to transform various industries and improve the efficiency and effectiveness of many processes by monitoring and control of the environment based on real-time data. However, they also present new challenges in terms of security, reliability, and privacy, as they are vulnerable to cyberattacks and other threats [1].

There are several methods that have been proposed to secure CPS. Some of these methods include encryption, network isolation, intrusion detection and prevention, vulnerability assessment, redundancy, and fail-safe measures. One of the methods that is widely being investigated is discussed in the following section.

6.2 Blockchain Technology in CPS

Blockchain technology presents a viable security solution for cyber-physical systems. Its decentralized and distributed nature renders it resistant to tampering and fraud, making it particularly suitable for safeguarding data transmission within CPS environments and ensuring system integrity. Additionally, blockchain facilitates secure and transparent transaction recording and was originally designed as the foundation for cryptocurrencies like Bitcoin. Figure 6.2 showcases the application of intelligent

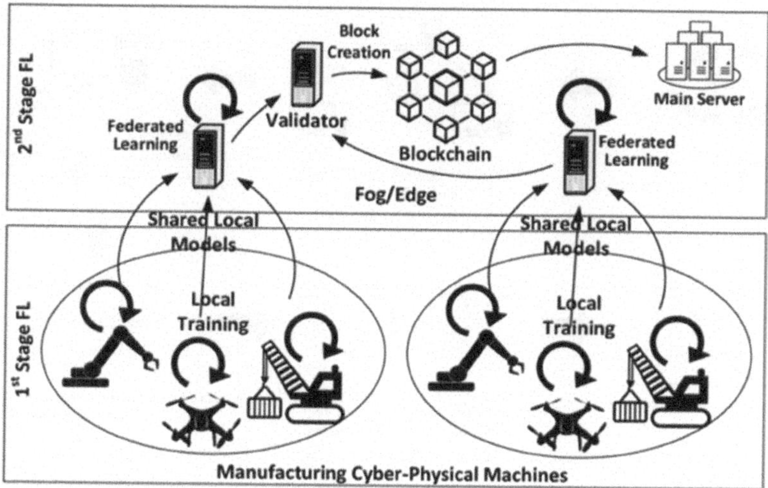

Fig. 6.2 Intelligent blockchain architecture for CPS [2]

blockchain technology in enhancing CPS security, offering protection against unauthorized access and tampering, while ensuring transparent transaction records. The benefits encompass reduced transaction costs, enhanced efficiency, and improved traceability and accountability.

6.2.1 How Blockchain Works

Blockchain technology functions as a decentralized and distributed system for managing accounting, facilitating secure and transparent transactions. Figure 6.3 provides a simplified depiction of blockchain's operation.

First, a user initiates a transaction, broadcasting it to the network, where it undergoes cryptographic verification before being added to a verified block along with other transactions. This block is subsequently appended to the blockchain, creating an immutable, linear chain of blocks, ensuring permanent, unalterable records.

6.2.2 Advantages and Disadvantages of Blockchain

Blockchain technology provides numerous advantages as a security measure when contrasted with alternative methods. Key benefits encompass decentralization, distributed nature, immutability, transparency, and efficiency, rendering it highly applicable across various security applications. Nonetheless, despite these advantages, it faces limitations and challenges, including scalability, energy consumption,

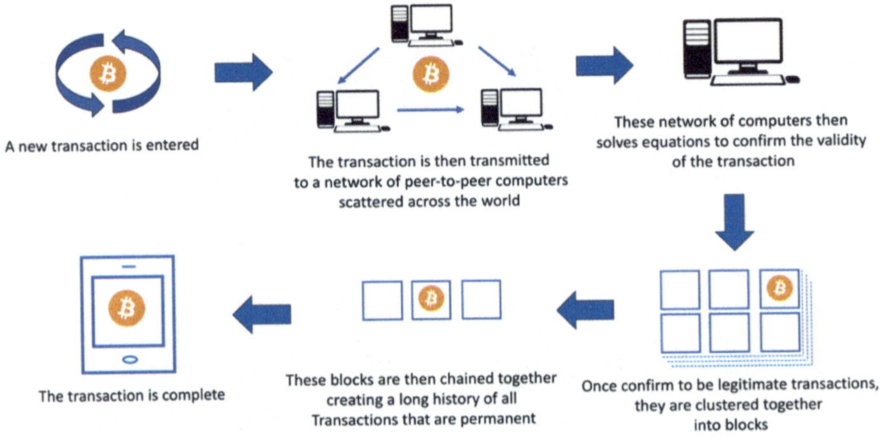

Fig. 6.3 Blockchain transaction process [3]

limited adoption, regulatory concerns, and security risks, which necessitate careful consideration.

6.2.3 Related Research on Blockchain for Security

In [4], research and design of power engineering project management using blockchain was proposed. The characteristics of electrical strength engineering initiatives, together with more than one type of multiple links, and decentralized construction have fashioned complex contracts and employment relationships. The blockchain-based totally electric power engineering challenge control gadget was designed. In addition, a cyber-manufacturing system (CMS) is proposed as a system that manages the manufacturing information that may exchange data among many parties through many devices over the computer network which needs a secure and transparent system during data exchange. This is where blockchain comes into a play. The CMS with blockchain is divided into four layers which are user layer, provider layer, service layer, and blockchain layer. The designed layers are being validate upon the security and safety level. The results of three different physical data audits are compared; the system's effectiveness is demonstrated [5].

Another study concerning food recalls and outbreaks has been done in [6] which discusses blockchain's ability for handling and monitoring product safety by keeping information ranging from product lifecycle, wholesale, logistics, standards, and certification. The focus of the study is the use of videogrammetry as an information collector on digital blockchain platforms. RFID and fingerprint combined with videogrammetry and blockchain solved the data verification issue.

Software-defined networks (SDN) with blockchain is a demanding field for investigation. With the huge number of nodes communicating in a network, the security concerns in SDN have become increasingly prominent. The SDN controller may not be able to manage controllers if the issue of secure and transparent communication is not being performed. As a result, intruders can attack with the flow table information of the AC machine. Therefore, the main security problems faced by SDN could be solved from multiple dimensions based on the decentralized, trustworthy, and self-willed characteristics of blockchain [7]. On the other hand, researchers in [8] have studied the overall status of the information security system based on the distributed and clustered characteristics of the blockchain. They also investigate the network information security mechanism under the blockchain technology.

Blockchain for CPS

Not surprisingly, blockchain could also be one of the promising solutions to enhance security in CPS. For instance, blockchain is largely used to assist Internet of Things technology operation in collecting and monitoring the environment in real time. Moreover, it is also highly used in (but not limited to) smart cities [9], supply chains, energy systems [10], smart health, automobile industry, and smart workspaces. CPS integration with blockchain can enhance its security level, dependability, and trust without the need to use a third party and controllers. Interestingly, blockchain can be used in tracking employees and objects used in their jobs for digital witnesses and monitoring purposes.

There are nine basic operations of blockchain in CPS, and the most common ones are command and control, sensing data acquisition, data communication, data storage, and coordination. Once data are acquired, they are typically logged (i.e., *data storage*) either directly or indirectly on the blockchain for persistency, forensic, and/or audit reasons. In addition, coordination among multiple participants is crucial in any networking system. In data acquisition, sensor data are protected using blockchain by identifying each user, and each data are transmitted with digital signatures to ensure data integrity. Access control of a network can also be benefited from blockchain using smart contract which can be applied across multiple entities [11]. Blockchain is also used in assisting a trust-management system which eliminates the use of the middleman, as shown in Fig. 6.4. Its decentralized nature and cryptographic algorithm make it more immune to attack and becomes more secure. The unique capability of blockchain for CPS enhanced the security and reliability that ensure data exchange is unsuspectingly for eavesdropping.

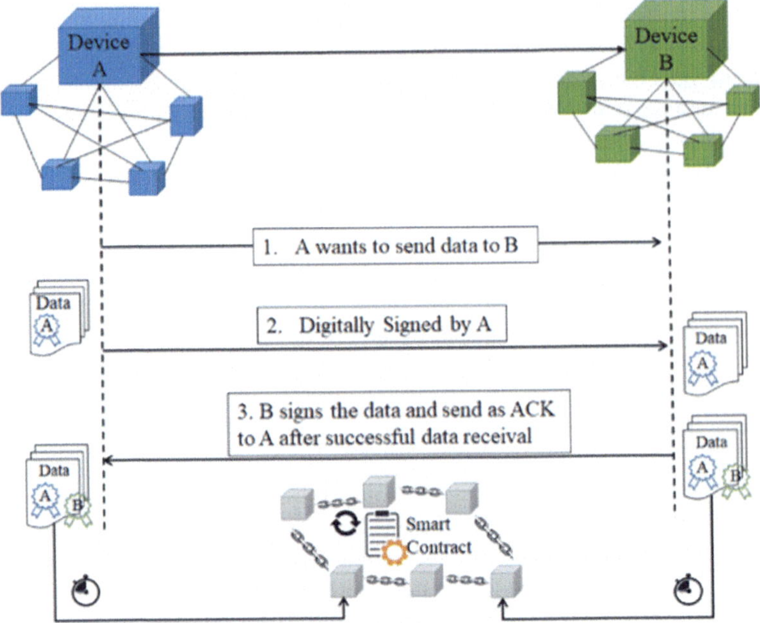

Fig. 6.4 Blockchain trust-management system in CPS [12]

6.3 Conclusion

This chapter has highlighted the significance of integrating blockchain into CPS. Blockchain technology has the potential to revolutionize many different industries, including the field of CPS. Some important areas where blockchain could have significant impact in the future of CPS research are supply chain management, data integrity, smart contracts, and identity and access management. Nevertheless, there is still much research to be done to understand the potential of blockchain in CPS.

References

1. Ch. K. Keerthi, M. A. Jabbar, B. Seetharamulu, Cyber physical systems (CPS):security issues, challenges and solutions. Paper presented at the 2017 IEEE International conference on computational intelligence and computing research (ICCIC), Coimbatore, India, 14–16 December 2017
2. M. Aloqaily, I. Al Ridhawi, F. Karray, M. Guizani, Towards Blockchain-based hierarchical federated learning for cyber-physical systems. Paper presented at the 5th International Balkan conference on communications and networking (BalkanCom), Sarajevo, Bosnia and Herzegovina, 22–24 August 2022
3. H. Adam, Blockchain facts: what is it, how it works, and how it can be used (Investopedia, 2023), https://www.investopedia.com/terms/b/blockchain.asp. Accessed 11 April 2023

4. Z. Shi, C. Kan, W. Tian, C. Liu, A Blockchain-based G-code protection approach for cyber-physical security in additive manufacturing. ASME. J. Comput. Inf. Sci. Eng. 21(4) (2021). https://doi.org/10.1115/1.4048966
5. J. Song, D. Shukla, M. Wu, V.V. Phoha, Y.B. Moon, Physical data auditing for attack detection in cyber-manufacturing systems: Blockchain for machine learning process. Paper presented at the ASME 2019 International mechanical engineering congress and exposition, Salt Lake City, USA, 11–14 November 2019
6. P.K. Gopalakrishnan, S. Behdad, A conceptual framework for using videogrammetry in blockchain platforms for food supply chain traceability. Paper presented at the 13th International conference on micro- and nanosystems, Anaheim, California, USA, 18–21 August 2019
7. L. Bai, L. Liu, Research on software defined network security model based on Blockchain. Paper Presented at the 6th International Conference on Intelligent computing and signal processing (ICSP), Xi'an, China, 9–11 April 2021
8. M.A. Rahman, M.M. Rashid, M.S. Hossain, E. Hassanain, M.F. Alhamid, M. Guizani, Blockchain and IoT-based cognitive edge framework for sharing economy services in a smart city. IEEE Access. **7**, 18611–18621 (2019). https://doi.org/10.1109/ACCESS.2019.2896065
9. A.S. Musleh, G. Yao, S.M. Muyeen, Blockchain applications in smart grid–review and frameworks. IEEE Access. **7**, 86746–86757 (2019). https://doi.org/10.1109/ACCESS.2019.2920682
10. Z. Gong-Guo, Z. Wan, Blockchain-based IoT security authentication system. Paper presented at the International conference on computer, blockchain and financial development (CBFD), Nanjing, China, 23–25 April 2021
11. P. Fraga-Lamas, T.M. Fernández-Caramés, A review on Blockchain technologies for an advanced and cyber-resilient automotive industry. IEEE Access. **7**, 17578–17598 (2019). https://doi.org/10.1109/ACCESS.2019.2895302
12. B.K. Mohanta, U. Satapathy, M.R. Dey, S.S. Panda, D. Jena, Trust management in cyber physical system using blockchain. Paper presented at the 11th International conference on computing, communication and networking technologies (ICCCNT), West Bengal, India, 1–3 July 2020

Chapter 7
Practiced-Based Research in New Media Design and Technology: Issues and Challenges in Designing Creative Outcome to Facilitate Learning

Zahidah Abd Kadir, Safurah Abdul Jalil, Bazilah A. Talip, and Puteri Nor Ellyza Nohuddin

Abstract Carrying out a research as a new media designer often takes the nature of practice called practice-based research. This approach allows researchers to have knowledge and understanding which may later lead to a successful design performance and improved acuity to designing and developing the creative outcomes. Revisiting the authors' previously published research work aims to provide more insights; the challenges and issues discussed in this chapter can be valuable in helping to design creative outcomes which can facilitate students' learning. This includes carefully planning the design thinking process as a creative approach that is iterative and encompasses methods and phases to show how new media designers think and work. The concept of practice-based research in this paper is one of the creative research exemplars to show how practice can inform research. Challenges and issues that are related to real-world experimentation setups to provide input for design education are also discussed. Hence, going through all the experiences faced by the authors, this chapter aims to share the essential information and knowledge which can be useful in designing research projects that apply practice-based research.

Z. A. Kadir (✉)
Higher Colleges of Technology, Sharjah Women's Campus, Sharjah, United Arab Emirates
e-mail: zabdkadir@hct.ac.ae

S. A. Jalil
Higher Colleges of Technology, Ras Al Khaimah Women's Campus, Ras Al Khaimah, United Arab Emirates
e-mail: sabduljalil@hct.ac.ae

B. A. Talip
Malaysian Institute of Information Technology, Universiti Kuala Lumpur, Kuala Lumpur, Malaysia
e-mail: bazilah@unikl.edu.my

P. N. E. Nohuddin
Higher Colleges of Technology, Sharjah, United Arab Emirates
e-mail: pnohuddin@hct.ac.ae

A. Ismail et al. (eds.), *Emerging Technologies and Sustainable Solutions*, SpringerBriefs in Applied Sciences and Technology,
https://doi.org/10.1007/978-3-032-18181-7_7

In this paper, the authors had revisited research work done in the field of new media design and technology for knowledge sharing contribution in terms of issues and challenges in designing creative outcomes to facilitate learning.

Keywords New media design and technology · Practice-based research · Creative design

7.1 Introduction

Carrying out a research as new media designers often takes the nature of practice called 'practice-based research'. This type of research gives rise to new concepts and methods that are generated from the original knowledge [1]. This is because research in the new media design and technology provides a platform that contributes to knowledge and design thinking in creative outcomes. The links between practice-based research and interdisciplinary research contribute to the field practice and utilize the essential services. For instance, researchers and practitioners or known as lab instructors, who apply a model of practice to a research study on the effectiveness of an augmented reality application in teaching and learning anatomy, might test the use of the application as an intervention among the undergraduate students to determine the application's effectiveness. The partnership between the researcher and practitioner had bridged the knowledge from basic to applied research. Concomitantly, the research process had benefited the practitioners, in which they can use the result to increase students' performance in learning anatomy, and simultaneously, the researchers were able to determine the design effectiveness of the augmented reality application. Therefore, the practice-based research approach had allowed the researcher to have knowledge and understanding which later led to a successful design performance and improved insights to designing and developing the creative outcome [2]. Taking careful steps in design planning is imperative to ensure that the impact of practice and strategy implementation can be maximized by the higher education institutions (HEIs) [3].

Designing creative outcomes to facilitate learning requires a careful instructional design approach and requires multimedia expertise. The encouragement of multimedia learning materials development using simple tools such as Microsoft PowerPoint to high-end software such as Adobe Animate and Adobe Articulate are among the authoring tools that are being used to develop the interactive content for design education. However, despite the fact that using new media design and technology are robust, research found that there is still insufficient content development, specifically in design education, to support the current needs in the teaching and learning process [3, 4]. This shows how important the design approach is because it requires careful planning for an appropriate development and interesting content for the multimedia learning material to be fully utilized. The use of multimedia learning materials as part of the new media design and technology have given users new experiences and interesting features which can be used to improve students' learning performance. Thus, it can be said that when a well-designed multimedia development is implemented properly, such materials have the potential to enhance learning. This new learning environment has changed the looks of how standard education setting, with teacher talk and paper-based materials for knowledge transmission, into a more authentic learning approach. With the new setting, the learners' needs and interests can be addressed appropriately, thus giving them learning autonomy that is more experiential and connected to the real world [5]. To design and develop a creative outcome for design education requires basic training, time and effort in order to take full advantage of the software application. Therefore, constructing an effective, useful, usable and satisfying content to facilitate learning is actually one of the main obstacles to be overcome because the design of learning is complex [4]. In response to this call, this paper aims to discuss the issues and challenges in designing creative outcomes to facilitate students' learning, which are presented through the selected case-study from the authors' previous research work.

7.2 Design Thinking Process

Design thinking is an iterative creative process that shows how designers think and work. Depending on the study, a creative project may use theories, models or frameworks from the design approach to address design challenges. Ideally, design thinking guides and supports creative ideation. It begins with the problem-solving stage that emulates with user engagement to reach a mutual understanding between designer/researcher and end user to define and create the relevant solution. In the previous research [6], the authors developed a multimedia learning material for physiotherapy. The study simulated a class of 130 students as the users to use the lab instructor's practical techniques in creating an effective solution for better learning performance. The techniques focused on users which assisted the instructional designer to understand the learning instructional and material needs by revealing what users did, valued and wanted [6].

Semi-structured interviews were also used to address the study objectives on students' and instructors' perceptions on teaching and learning current materials. For example, guided questions covered the desired subjects to gather thorough participant perspectives. Thus, this process ensured that learning issues were fully researched and feedbacks were comprehended. In addition, the study utilized a case-study technique to investigate multimedia learning in determining design criteria for effective learning products. Multimedia learning products have been lauded for their educational potential, but when the basic prerequisites are ignored, they may not succeed [7].

Normally, a researcher brainstorms and creates storyboard concepts and prototypes [8]. The problem-solving phase resources were incorporated into a guided multimedia storyboard development with specific tasks such as code programming, narrative and visual components of text, video, graphic and animation. Then, a prototype was built for users and teachers to use hands-on and provide appropriate comments during formative prototype assessment. In the final design process, the prototype was implemented, and a new media designer tested and evaluated the creative work. Subsequently, the users reviewed the prototype design to determine if it met the objectives. Finally, the testing phase was intended to find and fix usability issues in ongoing design. During development, design issues including inconsistent format, unclear directions, missing resources and bad style might be found. End users, peers and expert reviewers were invited to evaluate utilizing questionnaires to detect erroneous information through small group pilots, field testing, implementation and post-implementation interviews [7].

7.3 Creative Research Exemplar

This section defines the idea of practice-based research to show how practice can help research. Using the creation and development of cross-disciplinary multimedia learning tools for the physiotherapy program as examples, the creative result was meant to help and support students while they were learning in the practical lab. The design of learning is complicated, which makes it hard to come up with effective, useful, usable and satisfying content for digital learning materials [9]. To make sure that the video learning material is good, it is important to plan the style in detail [10]. This is because a design-oriented educational design model that uses practice-based research can cover all the teaching methods and settings that can be used to assist students to learn in design education. The quality of multimedia learning materials depends on how well they have been planned and arranged [10].

Through instructional design, learning goals can be met. Thus, it is very important to make sure the video learning materials are of high quality for a better way to teach and learn. The instructional design describes a full structure of the creation of instructional materials. In this study, the researcher made a full set of multimedia learning materials for the physiotherapy program's Basic Movement Therapy (BMT) course goals based on Galvis's educational design model [13]. The steps and activities in each of these stages made it possible to create the multimedia learning materials in a way that was easy to do. It also used the 'blended learning' method in face-to-face teaching. The idea of the design came from Galvis's [13] work, and the main design came from Clark and Mayer's [14] design guidance. Because of the classroom's size and time constraints, teaching practical skills is not the greatest. This did not define clinical challenges with physiotherapy education since active analysis during patient treatment required reordering practice skills [15].

A research was done to build successful multimedia learning aids utilizing the plan, prepare, produce and assess methodology [6]. To define the design criterion areas, content analysis was regarded as a critical stage prior to creation. Semi-structured interviews offered critical components for skill practice, notably in physiotherapy. During the planning phase, data were matched with multimedia design standards and content production was customized [14]. During the development phase, information was organized and a delivery system including instructional materials and activities to satisfy goals was created. The study demonstrated the effectiveness of digital learning resources and stressed the need of employing practice-based research methodologies to generate well-designed materials [16]. Analysing learners' requirements and goals, developing a delivery mechanism and measuring efficiency through continuous review were all part of the instructional design process [17]. The aim of the new media designer was to comprehend these processes and enhance learning results. The initial findings of the study were impacted by practice-based research.

7.4 Challenge in Creative Research

Testing the implementation of educational innovations in actual classroom settings rather than in sterile research laboratories/labs has become more common in practice-based research. Running the experiment in live classes has the benefit of allowing for a more accurate and realistic understanding of how the innovations function in actual classroom use. With new media approaches like digital game-based and gamified learning, where social influences are known to play a role in engaging some students with the activity, this particular benefit becomes a crucial criterion [11]. For instance, during an experiment on serious games conducted in a live course where students were playing the game simultaneously with their classmates [12], some students expressed how they were extremely motivated to get the highest score among their peers. These competitive students were observed to be willing to keep on playing and repeating the serious game until they accomplished their personal goal. Such observations may not have been possible or may yield different outcomes if the experiment is conducted in a controlled settings within a university research lab environment. Moreover, the complexity of instructional design [9] may mean that classroom gains observed in lab-based studies do not always translate to real-world situations.

Given that these experiments are typically carried out during actual classroom periods, the ethical principles and guidelines would differ from those conducted in isolated, controlled environments outside of formal learning period. As raised by [6], researchers conducting field experiments need to further assess their ethical implications and not simply adhere to ethical principles that are outdated or 'designed to protect and limit risk to individual participants in controlled laboratory settings'. Among ethical considerations would be to ensure that the experiment will not only address the research questions or satisfy the researcher's curiosity, but will also provide meaningful activities that will be beneficial for the students' academic development during the relevant classroom period that it intervenes. Therefore, the challenge lies in striking a balance so that the experiment will serve both the research study and the students taking part in it. The research activity should ideally be designed to blend seamlessly with the usual classroom learning activity, so that the students perceive the experiment session as one of their regular classes. Yet at the same time, ethical routines and procedures for real-world interventions such as getting students' consent, providing follow-ups and debriefing, should be embedded. Hence, working closely with the course instructor would be crucial.

Also, as highlighted by the first author earlier, it would be important to ensure the selected topic/learning content are in line with the particular course's planned syllabus and intended learning outcome at the early phase of the research design. This will help minimize any confounding variables that an experimental setting might unintentionally introduce to the study, or disruption to the learning period. However, testing a new technological intervention in a real-world educational setting and environment has its own set of challenges. In a controlled lab setting, individual participants can be closely watched and guided by the researcher. Real-world or field experiments usually lack such control, are inherently messy and can be unpredictable. Since it is more challenging to exercise the same level of control in real-world learning environments, the experiment setup necessitates different considerations.

In the case of the second author's research work, the technological intervention introduced in the classrooms was leveraging a game-based learning approach [7]. It is not uncommon for research to test proof of concepts using low-fidelity prototypes due to constraints of resources. However, using a low-fidelity prototype to evaluate the efficacy of an instructional strategy, such as game-based learning, may introduce unwanted effects, especially in an uncontrolled real-world learning environment. For instance, students might not be able to look past the crude implementation of the prototype, which in turn affects their overall learning experience. So, when students report not enjoying the GBL activity, it raises the question of whether it was due to the gameplay not being engaging or if it was due to the prototype failing to properly express the intended experience.

To minimize such distractions, while avoiding the substantial amount of time and resources that a complete high-fidelity prototype requires, the research proposed that a prototype with a 'vertical slice' quality is produced for technological interventions that are tested in real-world classrooms. Vertical slicing is one of the methods used in agile software development [8] where only a carefully selected 'slice' of the whole design was built into a high-fidelity, fully functional software with a quality that reflects the final product to be used in rapid, iterative testing. The 'vertical slice' method was found to offer a good way to guarantee that a substantial and complete chunk of the new learning application can be tested in a real-world course delivery setting. In particular to the published research work, the design and implementation of an interactive learning environment called *Design Eye* demonstrated how a modular learning approach for one of the visual elements of a GUI (i.e. colour) can be supported using an interactive instructional system. Another factor to be considered earlier on is the experiment's timing. Ideally, the experiment should be conducted during the class slot where the selected learning topic is supposedly covered in the semester. Unlike a lab-based study which can typically be conducted at any time that the researcher and participants are ready, a study involving a real-world experiment would need a more mindful planning when setting the research timeline. The researcher needs to note the semesters taking place at the HEIs where the experiment is to be conducted and identify the exact timeframe of the topic delivery based on the course syllabus.

A useful strategy is to plan in reverse once the date of the classroom experiment is determined, much like when working towards a deadline. In other words, start with determining the experiment date and then work backwards to develop the research plan to ensure that all phases of the prototype design are completed on time prior to the implementation. Of course, unforeseen issues can arise while completing the ongoing project. It is possible that development will not go as anticipated, the ethics review process might go beyond schedule, or bugs in the system may surface and require additional time to fix. These also need to be taken into account in order to accommodate for any potential unforeseen circumstances and provide for possible contingencies. Sometimes the topic covered by the research can still be moved to a slightly later week in the semester should an overshoot in the timeline happens, as long as delaying or swapping topics would not create any negative impact to students' learning. However, altering the timeline of an HEI's course delivery plan for the sake of the research is not desirable and should not be relied on as an option. An alternative option to counter the issue of missing the targeted timeframe would be to identify other similar courses across different HEIs as backups. The downside of using this strategy is that it will require additional time and effort to repeat the process of engaging with an HEI and ensuring that the research study likewise satisfy their specific learning requirements. Any differences between the courses or HEIs should also be noted and reported in the study.

As discussed by [10], researchers should be directed by their theoretical considerations when making methodological choices regarding the best type of research context given their area of interest. For example, in the context of design education, novice designers generally learn what works and what does not by reviewing the effects of the choices made, which makes the final product the result of this accumulation of design decisions. Using methods such as think-aloud can better capture data in regards to what design students were thinking as they, for example, choose the colours for their graphical user interface (GUI) as it allows for more in-depth understanding and better insights to students' thought processes. While a real-world experiment setup is good at capturing external validity, a lab-based setting may be better suited for such studies requiring internal validity as it enables clear causal inferences. Therefore, a researcher looking to conduct an educational research study may want to consider supplementing their work in a real-world experiment setup with lab-based studies to cater for their research needs.

7.5 Conclusion

In this contribution, the paper proposes the definition of a practice-based approach in creative research and practice from the dimension of design thinking approach, the exemplar of a creative research project and issues and challenges in creative research. The authors underline how practice informs the research when the practice-based approach is applied specifically in the new media design and technology to facilitate learning. Apart from that, the paper discussed the challenges encountered by the researcher in terms of real-world experimentation setup and issues arising during data collection that used the qualitative methodology. The contribution of knowledge in this paper is based on the authors' previous published research in designing creative outcomes to facilitate the learning.

References

1. I. Magrin-Chagnolleau, Reflections on the impact of creation research, practice-based research, and practice as research, and how to define and maximize that impact. Media Pract. Educ. **23**(2), 105–111 (2022). https://doi.org/10.1080/25741136.2022.2058864
2. L. Candy, *Practice Based Research: A Guide* (Sydney, 2014)
3. K. Lonka, V. Cho, Innovative schools in digital era. Eur. Parlam. **78** (2015)
4. M. Hamdi, T. Hamtini, Designing an effective e-content development framework for the enhancement of learning programming. Int. J. Emerg. Technol. Learn. **11**(4), 131–141 (2016). https://doi.org/10.3991/ijet.v11i04.5574
5. B. Cope, M. Kalantzis, Towards a new learning: the scholar social knowledge workspace, in theory and practice. E-Learn. Digit. Media **10**(4), 332–356 (2013). https://doi.org/10.2304/elea.2013.10.4.332
6. R. McDermott, P.K. Hatemi, Ethics in field experimentation: A call to establish new standards to protect the public from unwanted manipulation and real harms. **117**(48), 30014–30021 (2020). https://doi.org/10.1073/pnas.2012021117
7. S. Abdul Jalil, Instructional strategies for the visual aesthetics of user interface design incorporating game-based learning into a modular multi-structural approach. Ph.D thesis, University of Auckland (2015)
8. T. Myklebust, T. Stålhane, *Functional Safety and Proof of Compliance* (Springer Cham, 2022)
9. K.R. Koedinger, J.L. Booth, D. Klahr, Instructional complexity and the science to constrain it. **342**, 935–937 (2013). https://doi.org/10.1126/science.1238056
10. G.A. Holleman, I.T.C. Hooge, C. Kemner, R.S. Hessels, The 'real-world approach' and its problems: a critique of the term ecological validity. **11** (2020). https://doi.org/10.3389/fpsyg.2020.00721
11. C.-H. Chen, G.-J. Hwang, Effects of the team competition-based ubiquitous gaming approach on students' interactive patterns, collective efficacy and awareness of collaboration and communication. Educ. Technol. Soc. **20**(1), 87–98 (2017) http://www.jstor.org/stable/jeductechsoci.20.1.87
12. S. Abdul Jalil, B. Plimmer, I. Warren, A. Luxton-Reilly, Exploring serious mini-games for enhancing computing students' colour selection skills, in *Proceedings of EdMedia + Innovate Learning*, ed. by J. Viteli, M. Leikomaa, (Association for the Advancement of Computing in Education (AACE), Waynesville, NC, June 2014), pp. 2096–2106
13. A.T. Galvis, in Computer-Assisted Instruction (Cai) As A Teaching Tool for Occupational Therapy Education: A Guide to Understand Cai Design and Effectiveness, issue May (Texas Woman's University, 2007)
14. R.C. Clark, R.E. Mayer, in E-Learning and the Science of Instruction: Proven Guidelines for Consumers and Designers of Multimedia Learning, 3rd edn., issue September (Pfeiffer, Hoboken, NJ, USA, 2011)
15. M. Rowe, J. Frantz, V. Bozalek, The role of blended learning in the clinical education of healthcare students: a systematic review. Med. Teach. **34**(4), e216–21 (2012). https://doi.org/10.3109/0142159X.2012.642831

16. Z.A. Kadir, S.B. Baboo, N.S. Rosni, Z.H. Abd Rahman, N. Abu Bakar, Digital learning resource for basic movement therapy course: blended learning approach. Pertanika J. Sci. Technol. **25**(S5), 9–16 (2017)
17. K.A. Kallio, Instructional design. Res. Starters–Educ. 2000 (April), 1–81 (2017). http://www.nwlink.com/~donclark/hrd/learning/development.html

Chapter 8
Design and Development of Android-Based Gesture Recognition System for Deaf-Mute Individuals

Ku Nurul Fazira Ku Azir, Adam Mohd Khairuddin, Mohd Rashidi Che Beson, and Abdul Rahman Al Hafiz Abdul Rahim

Abstract This research attempted to classify 15 types of gestures to communicate between normal people and deaf-mute individuals by implementing an Android-based gesture recognition system. The gesture recognition system was developed using an ESP32 microcontroller, flex sensor, MPU 6050 accelerometer, and Android application. The performance of the Android-based gesture recognition system as developed in this study was able to achieve an average accuracy (ACC) of 90.80% when evaluated with deaf-mute individuals.

Keywords Recognition · Communication · Android · Accelerometer · Sensor

8.1 Introduction

Sign language can be defined as manual communication used by deaf-mute individuals [1]. Deaf-mute individuals from various countries around the world speak different sign languages with unique gestures or symbols. Each gesture is known as

K. N. F. Ku Azir (✉) · M. R. Che Beson
Centre of Excellence for Advanced Computing, Faculty of Intelligent Computing, Universiti Malaysia Perlis, Arau, Perlis, Malaysia
e-mail: fazira@unimap.edu.my

M. R. Che Beson
e-mail: rashidibeson@unimap.edu.my

A. Mohd Khairuddin
Department of Intelligence Informatics, Faculty of Artificial Intelligence, Universiti Teknologi Malaysia, Kuala Lumpur, Federal Territory of Kuala Lumpur, Malaysia
e-mail: adam.mk@utm.my

A. R. A. H. Abdul Rahim
Faculty of Electronic Engineering & Technology, Universiti Malaysia Perlis, Arau, Perlis, Malaysia
e-mail: abdulrahmanhafiz@gmail.com

A. Ismail et al. (eds.), *Emerging Technologies and Sustainable Solutions*, SpringerBriefs in Applied Sciences and Technology,
https://doi.org/10.1007/978-3-032-18181-7_8

a sign. There are three distinct parts of gestures: (1) hand shape, (2) hand position, and (3) hand movement.

In Malaysia, Bahasa Isyarat Malaysia (BIM) and Malaysian Sign Language (MSL) are the primary means of communication among the deaf-mute community in Malaysia [2]. According to [3], 40,743 hearing-impaired adults and children have been registered in Malaysia as of December 31, 2021. Unfortunately, deaf-mute people are considered vulnerable groups that face difficulties connecting themselves with non-deaf individuals [4]. The communication gap often leaves the deaf-mute person socially excluded or isolated at school or work. It is also suggested that poor communication affects the deaf community, causing them to have higher rates of anxiety, depression, and emotional distress than the general population. Hence, more attention should be paid to support the deaf-mute community.

Over the years, various gesture systems have been proposed to improve communication barriers, increase well-being, and offer a better sense of belonging to the deaf-mute community in Malaysia. For instance, a recent study [5] proposed an interactive virtual reality (VR) website as a learning platform to help deaf-mute children. This VR website provides graphical content that allows children to learn by watching videos, answering quizzes, and playing games. The results of this study indicate that the proposed VR website can achieve an acceptance rate of more than 80.00%.

The importance of adopting a gesture system to classify different sign languages has been emphasized in previous studies. Nonetheless, previous studies have also suggested that there are limitations in terms of power consumption, high operating cost, and low-resolution images. Therefore, there is a need to develop a gesture recognition system that can classify sign languages. The development of the Android-based gesture recognition system involved the use of a flex sensor, MPU 6050 accelerometer, ESP32 microcontroller, and Android application.

8.2 Methodology

The development of the Android-based gesture recognition system in this study included the following two important stages: (1) hardware design and (2) software design.

8.2.1 Hardware Design

The hardware design of the system is related to the development of an assistive glove. The assistive glove comprises the following four hardware components. These components included (1) an ESP32 microcontroller, (2) a flex sensor, (3) an MPU 6050 accelerometer, and (4) a 9 V power supply.

ESP32 Microcontroller

The ESP32 microcontroller is a low-cost system-on-chip (SoC) microcontroller developed by Espressif Systems. It has bluetooth and Wi-Fi functionalities. The ESP32 microcontroller was selected to process the gesture data received from both the flex sensors and the MPU 6050 accelerometer before transmitting the processed gesture data to the Android application.

Flex Sensor

The flex sensor measured the amount of deflection and bending. In this study, five flex sensors were used to develop an assistive glove. This is because five flex sensors were used to collect the threshold values of the flex sensor from every digit of the hand: (1) thumb, (2) index, (3) middle, (4) ring, and (5) little.

MPU 6050 Accelerometer

An MPU 6050 accelerometer was also used to develop the assistive glove. The MPU 6050 accelerometer is a motion-tracking device used to track the angular motion and acceleration of an object. It combines a 3-axis gyroscope and a 3-axis accelerometer on the same silicon die. This device was used to collect the threshold values of the accelerometer from each digit of the hand.

8.2.2 Software Design

The software design of the system involved the development of an Android application to detect and classify hand gestures from an assistive glove. Two types of software were used: (1) Arduino IDE v1 and (2) MIT App Inventor.

Arduino IDE v1

The Arduino integrated development environment or Arduino software (IDE) includes a text editor to write and upload code to the Arduino boards. In this work, a sketch was written to collect the threshold values of the flex sensors and accelerometer when gestures were performed using the established connection between the assistive gloves.

MIT App Inventor

The MIT App Inventor is a visual web programming environment used to build fully functional apps for android-based devices. In this study, an Android application to detect 15 types of gestures was developed using the MIT App Inventor. Live testing was performed using a software emulator installed on a computer. This was to test whether the functionality of the Android application could work as intended with the assistive glove.

8.3 Experimental Setup

An experiment to evaluate the performance of the Android-based gesture recognition system was carried out by both deaf and non-deaf people. Two different parameters were used to evaluate the performance of the system in categorizing the 15 types of sign languages: (1) hand size of the participants and (2) ability of the flex sensor to detect finger bending per second.

The experiment for deaf people was conducted at Politeknik Tuanku Syed Sirajuddin, Perlis, Malaysia. Five different participants with distinct hand sizes were selected to evaluate the system performance. The participants wore the glove and performed gestures for all the 15 types of sign languages. To ensure a high accuracy, all gestures were performed within a given time delay of 3.5 s. All gestures for each sign language were executed and repeated ten times.

The experiment for non-deaf people was carried out at the Universiti Malaysia Perlis, Malaysia. Five participants with different hand sizes were selected. The non-deaf wore the glove and performed the gestures for all 15 types of sign languages. All gestures in each sign language were executed and repeated 15 times.

The findings of this study were evaluated by using the accuracy (ACC) metric. The accuracy (ACC) metric was used to evaluate the performance of the Android-based gesture recognition system in detecting 15 types of sign languages.

8.4 Results and Discussion

The threshold values of the flex sensor and accelerometer values that were produced were dependent on the type of sign language performed by the assistive glove. The flex sensor had five threshold values, whereas the accelerometer had three values. To achieve high accuracy when using the assistive glove, the threshold values of both the flex sensor and accelerometer must fall within a specific range of threshold values.

The Android application was also evaluated by inputting the test values of the flex sensors for each digit of the hand (1) thumb; (2) index; (3) middle; (4) ring; and (5) little. Table 8.1 illustrates the different types of hand gestures performed by users using the assistive glove with their respective messages generated by the Android application. Based on the results in Table 8.1, all 15 types of gestures were able to correctly display messages on the Android application when tested using the proposed Android-based gesture recognition system.

Figure 8.1 illustrates the accuracy (ACC) of the system in categorizing all 15 types of gestures when tested by deaf-mute individuals. The results in Fig. 8.1 show that three types of gestures (hello, okay, and library) were able to achieve an accuracy (ACC) of 100.00% when evaluated by all users (A, B, C, D, and E). However, there are 12 types of gestures that can yield an accuracy of less than 100%. The gesture (Where is the toilet?) achieved the lowest accuracy (ACC) of 68.00%.

Table 8.1 Illustration of gestures performed by the user using the assistive glove and their respective messages generated by the Android application

Message	Gestures	Display	Message	Gestures	Display
Hello		connected Hai	Call the police station		connected Call Police Station
Welcome		connected Welcome	Thank you		connected Thank you
Pardon me		connected Pardon Me	Call the fire station		connected Call Firestation
I love you		connected I love you	Come here		connected Come Here
Okay		connected Okay	Call ambulance		connected Call Ambulance
Need help		connected Need Help	Library		connected Library
Home		connected Home	I need medicine		connected I need medicine
Where is the toilet?		connected Where the toilet?			

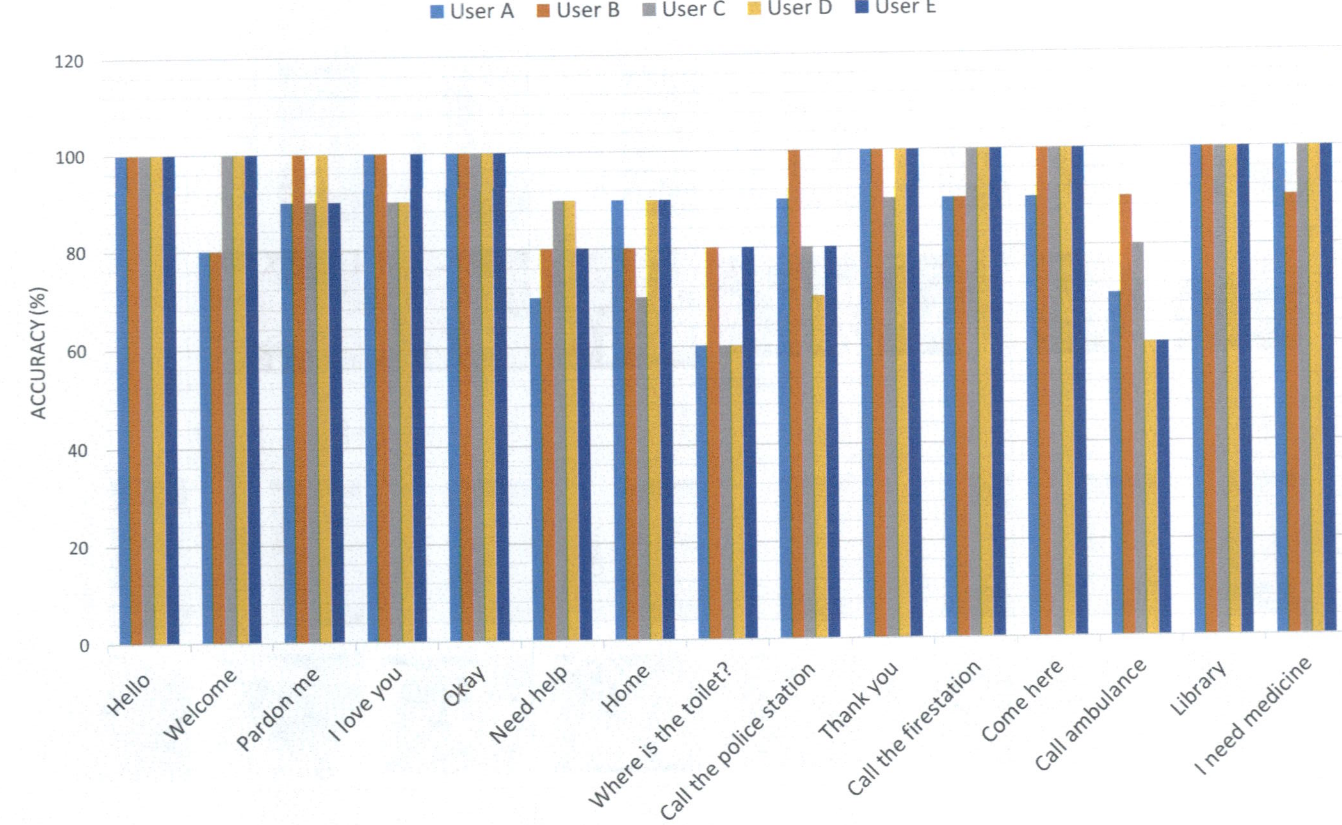

Fig. 8.1 The accuracy (ACC) of the Android-based gesture recognition system when evaluated by deaf individuals

The system achieved the accuracy (ACC) of 88.67%, 92.67%, 90.00%, 90.67%, 92.00%, and 90.80% when evaluated by users A, B, C, D, and E, respectively. The system yielded the highest accuracy of 92.67% when evaluated by user B. The lowest accuracy of 88.67% was achieved when tested by user A. Nonetheless, the difference in the performance of the proposed Android-based gesture recognition system may be due to the following factors: (1) Flexibility of the flex sensor may be degraded after undergoing long period of testing; (2) Loose attachment of flex sensors on the glove can affect stability; (3) Different value of temperature (high/low) can affect values during testing; and (4) size of fingers (longer finger will exert more bending force). Overall, the proposed Android-based gesture recognition system achieved an average accuracy (ACC) of 90.80% when tested on all five deaf individuals.

8.5 Conclusion

This work attempted to classify 15 types of different types of hand gestures by utilizing an Android-based gesture recognition system that was implemented based on a flex sensor, 3-axis accelerometer, bluetooth module, and mobile application. Normal and non-deaf people were involved in evaluating the performance of the system. According to the results of this study, the Android-based gesture recognition system developed was able to yield an average accuracy (ACC) of 90.80% when tested with deaf-mute individuals. For future research, it is suggested that more flex sensors are added to other parts of the body (arm, elbow, and shoulder) to increase the accuracy of the system. It is also suggested that the notification system and GPS tracking function be integrated into a system that can be used by emergency services (police stations, hospitals, fire stations) to enhance the safety of disabled people whenever they are in a distress situation.

References

1. V.T. Mueller, American sign language (ASL), in *Encyclopedia of Autism Spectrum Disorders*, ed. by F. Volkmar, (Springer, New York, 2019), pp. 1–4
2. A. Wadhawan, P. Kumar, Sign language recognition systems: a decade systematic literature review. Arch. Comput. Methods Eng. **28**, 785–813 (2021). https://doi.org/10.1007/s11831-019-09384-2
3. W. Muthiah, Over 40,000 hearing-impaired people registered in Malaysia. The Star Online (2022). https://www.thestar.com.my/news/nation/2022/03/03/kj-over-40000-hearing-impaired-people-registered-in-malaysia. Accessed 10 Mar 2023
4. W.Y. Lee, J.T.A. Tan, J.K. Kok, The struggle to fit in: a qualitative study on the sense of belonging and well-being of deaf people in Ipoh, Perak, Malaysia. Psychol. Stud. **67**, 385–400 (2022). https://doi.org/10.1007/s12646-022-00658-7
5. N.R. Rahim, R.A.A. Abdul, A virtual reality approach to support Malaysian sign language interactive learning for deaf-mute children. J. Pharm. Negat. Results. **13**, 4962–4974 (2022). https://doi.org/10.47750/pnr.2022.13.S07.614

Chapter 9
Geometrical Parameters Optimization of a Square Micro Coil Using a Two-Level Factorial Technique

Norliana Yusof, Noor Hidayah Mohd Yunus, Badariah Bais, Siti Amalina Enche Ab Rahim, Tuan Norjihan Tuan Yaakub, and Mohamad Nur Fuadi Pargi

Abstract This paper presents a statistical design method that provides a better optimization for design parameter values of a square micro coil. Computer Simulation Technology (CST) software is used in this study to build and simulate the micro coil structure. The influence of a square micro coil's geometrical parameters namely, its outer diameter, frequency response, and quality factor on the intended output was examined using the statistical two-level factorial technique. From the study, the number of turns of the micro coil is the dominating factor for all targeted output. The results showed that the coil width of 31 μm, gap of 50 μm, thickness of 30 μm, number of turns of 33, and inner diameter of 1294 μm are most preferable to optimize

N. Yusof · M. N. F. Pargi
Faculty of Innovative Design and Technology, Universiti Sultan Zainal Abidin, Kuala Nerus, Terengganu, Malaysia
e-mail: norliana@unisza.edu.my

M. N. F. Pargi
e-mail: mohamadnurfuadi@unisza.edu.my

N. H. M. Yunus (✉)
Advanced Telecommunication Technology, Communication Technology Section, British Malaysian Institute, Universiti Kuala Lumpur , Gombak, Selangor, Malaysia
e-mail: noorhidayahm@unikl.edu.my

B. Bais
Department of Electrical, Electronic and Systems Engineering, Faculty of Engineering and Built Environment, Universiti Kebangsaan Malaysia, Bangi, Selangor, Malaysia
e-mail: badariah@ukm.edu.my

S. A. E. A. Rahim
Microwave Research Institute, Universiti Teknologi Mara, Shah Alam, Selangor, Malaysia
e-mail: amalinaabr@uitm.edu.my

T. N. T. Yaakub
School of Electrical Engineering, College of Engineering, Universiti Teknologi Mara, Shah Alam, Selangor, Malaysia
e-mail: tuan_norjihan@uitm.edu.my

A. Ismail et al. (eds.), *Emerging Technologies and Sustainable Solutions*, SpringerBriefs in Applied Sciences and Technology,
https://doi.org/10.1007/978-3-032-18181-7_9

the targeted output. The prediction of multi-response using optimized values gives a quality factor, frequency response, and outer diameter of 68.69, 57.59–64.14 MHz, and 5999 μm, respectively. The two-level factorial technique was able to predict the optimum micro coil parameters with minimal error, demonstrated by the difference between the verified value and the anticipated value being within the range of 1.16–8.56%. The optimization results showed that the predicted geometrical parameters can be employed to achieve the target specifications for pressure monitoring application.

Keywords Optimization · Quality factor · Design of experiment · MEMS · Sensor

9.1 Introduction

The interest in the development of inductive-capacitive (LC) micro-electro-mechanical systems (MEMS) pressure sensor has increased due to its potential applications in many field. The majority of the MEMS pressure sensors were developed using the LC actuation mechanism to convert pressure into an electrical signal due to its low noise, low power consumption, low temperature, and significant sensitivity to pressure variations [1]. Most importantly, it could be integrated easily with passive telemetry electronics which is requiring no incorporated battery [2]. High sensitivity and quality factor (Q-factor) are important parameters in designing an efficient wireless MEMS capacitive pressure sensor. The quality factor measures the energy transmission efficiency of an LC resonant sensor. To achieve a high quality factor, the coil needs to have high self-inductance and low series resistance as shown in Eq. (9.1) [3], [4].

$$Q = \frac{\omega.L}{R} \tag{9.1}$$

where ω_O, L, and R are the angular resonant frequency ($\omega_0 = 2\pi f$), self-inductance, and resistance of the coil, respectively. The resonance frequency of the LC-sensor is given by Eq. (9.2) [3, 4].

$$f = \frac{1}{2\pi}\sqrt{\frac{1}{LC}} \tag{9.2}$$

Toward designing a minimally invasive implantable pressure sensor, an investigation and optimization of geometrical parameters of the micro coil should be well conducted [5]. This micro coil can be integrated with a MEMS pressure sensor for inductive wireless coupling [1, 3, 6]. An effective approach in optimization of multi-response is the design of experiment (DOE) method. There are five geometrical parameters on the square micro coil that needs to be controlled, namely the width, gap, thickness, number of turns, and inner diameter. The targeted output includes high quality factor, high sensitivity, range of operating between 10–100 MHz and overall size not more than 6 mm. The targeted output is selected according to the design specifications for bladder implants application. The diameter of human intra-urethral is 7–8 mm [7]; hence, the maximum size of outer diameter of the micro coil is chosen to be not more than 6 mm after taking into consideration the sensor packaging. Meanwhile, the suitable operating frequency relies in the range of 10–100 MHz for in-vivo wireless measurements [8].

9.2 Methodology

Computer Simulation Technology (CST) software is suitable for electromagnetic, antenna, micro coil design, and other related fields [9]. In this study, the micro coil was designed and simulated using a CST software by employing finite element analysis (FEA) to predict the behavior of the micro coil and optimize its performance. FEA method and design of experiment (DOE) method are presented in this section.

9.2.1 *Finite Element Analysis Method*

The designed micro coil structure was the same as in our previous study [5]. In this study, FEA method is used to obtain the targeted output, namely the quality factor (Q-factor) and outer diameter. The simulation data were then coupled with the analytical methods to calculate the frequency response ($F_{\min}$ and $F_{\max}$). The DOE method was based on FEA simulation data and was used for the prediction of optimized parameters and the investigation of effect geometric parameters on the targeted output.

9.2.2 *Design of Experiment Method*

The Design Expert Statistical Software (Stat-Ease, USA) is used to study the effect of geometrical parameters and predict the optimized geometrical parameters of the square micro coil. All design parameters including the experimental ranges of square micro coil are shown in Table 9.1. The range of the geometrical parameters (controlled factors) is based on previous research [3, 10, 11]. Through this DOE process, the interactions of these parameters and their impact on the targeted output can be derived. Next, optimization of design parameters was conducted to achieve the targeted output as shown in Table 9.2.

Table 9.1 Control parameters level and their respective codes

Code	Control parameters	Low level (μm)	High level (μm)
A	Coil width	30	50
B	Coil gap	10	50
C	Coil thickness	1	30
D	Number of turns	20	50
E	Inner diameter	500	1300

Table 9.2 Targeted output of optimization

Output	Target
Q factor	Maximum
Minimum frequency, F_{min}	$\geq$10 MHz
Maximum frequency, F_{max}	$\leq$100 MHz
Outer diameter, D_{out}	$\leq$ 6000 μm

9.3 Results and Discussion

This section presents the FEA results from CST simulation and DOE. The percent of contribution for each factor and predicted optimal design parameters of micro coil were analyzed and discussed.

9.3.1 *Finite Element Analysis Results*

The targeted output for different combinations of the control parameters, is obtained using the CST software based on the FEA simulations. The inner coil is connected to the outer coil by $Z = 50\ \Omega$ port. The inductance and Q-factor value were collected due to the changes of the coil geometry. Then, the inductance value was analyzed to calculate minimum and maximum frequency by using Eq. (9.2). The capacitive analysis was referred to our previous study [12, 13] by applying a pressure of 0–160 mmHg on the slotted diaphragm. From the study, the optimized capacitance changes is in between 2.11 pF and 2.70 pF [13].

9.3.2 *Design of Experiment Results*

One interesting analysis utilized by two-level factorial approach is to calculate the percentage contribution of each parameter to the targeted output as shown Fig. 9.1. From Fig. 9.1, the number of turns gives the highest contribution to the Q-factor, outer diameter, and frequency response with 67%, 64%, and 93% percent contribution,

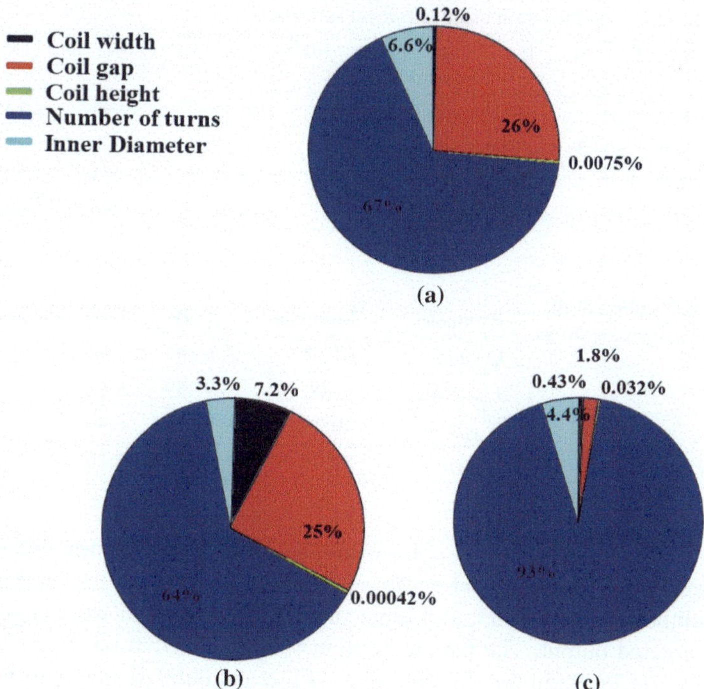

Fig. 9.1 Percent contribution for **a** Q factor **b** outer diameter **c** frequency

respectively. Increasing the number of turns, increases the inductance of the coil, and lowered the frequency response, which leads to an increased value of Q-factor and outer diameter of the micro coil. This finding is also in agreement with research conducted by Yunas et al. 2010 [14]. Meanwhile, Fig. 9.1 also reveals that coil gap, B gives high effect to the Q factors and outer diameter compared to the other factors with 26% and 25% percent contribution, respectively. In addition, the coil height is found to be a non-significant factor for all targeted outputs.

9.3.3 Multi-response Optimization Results

The optimization of design parameters of a square micro coil was performed with the aim of obtaining the maximum Q-factor, maximum sensitivity (significance difference between F_{min} and F_{max}), and outer diameter not exceeding 6000 μm. During the optimization selection process, the targeted output was set at the following conditions: Q-factor was set at maximum, F_{max} at maximum within range less than 100 MHz, F_{min} at minimum within range more than 10 MHz, and the outer diameter were set within range up to 6000 μm. Table 9.3 shows the best four optimization

Table 9.3 Results of optimization using two-level factorial

Run	A	B	C	D	E	Q Factor	F_{min} (MHz)	F_{max} (MHz)	D_{out} (μm)	Desirability
1	31.0	50.0	30.0	33.0	1294.0	68.69	57.59	64.14	5999	0.558
2	30.0	50.0	30.0	35.1	974.7	68.07	57.37	64.57	6000	0.558
3	30.0	50.0	30.0	34.6	968.5	67.53	58.45	65.82	5923	0.557
4	30.0	49.9	30.0	36.3	779.1	67.26	57.33	64.98	5999	0.556

Table 9.4 Verification of the predicted optimum conditions

Parameter	Simulation	DOE	Deviation error (%)
Q factor	67.37	68.69	1.96
F_{min}(MHz)	53.00	57.59	8.66
F_{max}(MHz)	59.95	64.14	6.99
D_{out}(μm)	5930	5999	1.16

results for the targeted output. The optimization results showed a desirability of 0.558. The optimized conditions of coil width = 31 μm, coil gap = 50 μm, coil height = 30 μm, number of turns = 33, and inner diameter = 1294 μm were suggested to meet the targeted output. The targeted output was predicted at 68.69, 57.59 MHz, 64.14 MHz, and 5999 μm for Q-factor, F_{max}, F_{min}, and outer diameter, respectively. Once again, FEA simulation by CST has been conducted to estimate this optimized geometrical parameter. The validated results between simulation and predicted by two-level factorial is shown in Table 9.4. The results showed a close agreement indicating the satisfactoriness of the obtained model to optimize design parameters with deviation error within 1.16–8.66%. To achieve a reliable statistical analyses, the deviation error values must be less than 20% [15]. Therefore, the model generated from two-level factorial technique is reliable and suitable for predicting the geometrical parameters to achieve the targeted output.

9.4 Conclusion

The implementation of DOE-based design optimization for a square micro coil is presented. Geometrical parameters of a square micro coil are optimized using two-level fractional factorial design. The DOE technique results, which were verified via FEA-based simulations, indicated a close agreement. This suggests that statistical DOE-based methodology for MEMS devices is efficient and feasible for the purpose of multi response optimization. The effects of geometrical parameters and their impact on the targeted output can be well analyzed and understood, thus useful as a guideline for future successful fabrication of MEMS devices.

References

1. Q.A. Huang, L. Dong, L.F. Wang, LC passive wireless sensors toward a wireless sensing platform: Status, prospects, and challenges. J. Microelectromech. Syst. **25**(5), 822–841 (2016)
2. H. Cao, U. Tata, V. Landge, A.L. Li, Y.B. Peng, J.C. Chiao, A wireless bladder volume monitoring system using a flexible capacitance-based sensor, in *2013 IEEE Topical Conference on Biomedical Wireless Technologies, Networks, and Sensing Systems*, (IEEE, 2013), pp. 34–36
3. J. Zhai, T.V. How, B. Hon, Design and modelling of a passive wireless pressure sensor. CIRP Ann. **59**(1), 187–190 (2010)
4. C.R. Neagu, H.V. Jansen, A. Smith, J.G.E. Gardeniers, M.C. Elwenspoek, Characterization of a planar micro coil for implantable microsystems. Sens Actuators Phys. **62**(1–3), 599–611 (1997)
5. N. Yusof, S.M. Norzeli, S.N.A. Yusof, N.H.M. Yunus, N. Soin, Modeling and simulation of planar micro-coils for invasive pressure sensing, in *Advancements in Materials Science and Technology Led by Women*, (Springer, New York, 2023), pp. 165–172
6. J. Park, J.K. Kim, S.J. Patil, J.K. Park, S. Park, D.W. Lee, A wireless pressure sensor integrated with a biodegradable polymer stent for biomedical applications. Sensors **16**(6), 809 (2016)
7. W.S. McDougal, A.J. Wein, L.R. Kavoussi, A.W. Partin, C.A. Peters, *Campbell-Walsh Urology 11th Edition Review E-Book* (Elsevier Health Sciences, 2015)
8. M. Luo, A.W. Martinez, C. Song, F. Herrault, M.G. Allen, A microfabricated wireless RF pressure sensor made completely of biodegradable materials. J. Microelectromech. Syst. **23**(1), 4–13 (2013)
9. J. Yunas et al., Design and fabrication of glass based mems patch antenna for energy harvester, in *2020 IEEE International Conference on Power and Energy (PECon)*, (IEEE, 2020), pp. 362–365
10. O. Akar, T. Akin, K. Najafi, A wireless batch sealed absolute capacitive pressure sensor. Sens Actuators Phys. **95**(1), 29–38 (2001)
11. N. Xue, S.P. Chang, J.B. Lee, A SU-8-based microfabricated implantable inductively coupled passive RF wireless intraocular pressure sensor. J. Microelectromech. Syst. **21**(6), 1338–1346 (2012)
12. N. Yusof, B. Bais, B.Y. Majlis, N. Soin, Mechanical analysis of MEMS diaphragm for bladder pressure monitoring, in *2017 IEEE Regional Symposium on Micro and Nanoelectronics (RSM)*, (IEEE, 2017), pp. 22–25
13. N. Yusof, B. Bais, B.Y. Majlis, N. Soin, Sensitivity and Q-factor trade-off analysis of MEMS pressure sensor for bladder implants, in *2018 IEEE 8th international nanoelectronics conferences (INEC)*, (IEEE, 2018), pp. 49–50
14. J. Yunas, N. Sulaiman, G. Sugandi, A.A. Hamzah, B.Y. Majlis, Geometrical analysis of planar coil design for fluxgate magnetometer. Microsyst. **16**, 1939–1944 (2010)
15. M.H. Cetin, B. Ozcelik, E. Kuram, E. Demirbas, Evaluation of vegetable based cutting fluids with extreme pressure and cutting parameters in turning of AISI 304L by Taguchi method. J. Clean. Prod. **19**(17–18), 2049–2056 (2011)

Chapter 10
Impact of COVID-19 on Software Development Life Cycle

Ayesha Anees Zaveri, Juliana Jaafar, and Eid Yafi

Abstract In 2020, COVID-19 affected nearly every industry, including IT. The pandemic compelled millions of employees to work from home. Modern IT tools, networks, and infrastructure have enabled remote work and contributed to the containment of the pandemic. Some businesses struggled to adopt remote work during the pandemic. Due to the numerous advantages of teleworking, software development will help global businesses manage their workforces and increase productivity with remote digital tools. Therefore, it is essential to strategically improve the software development process when requirements are ambiguous or rapidly changing.

Keywords COVID-19 · Pandemic · Software development life cycle · Software engineering · Information technology

10.1 Introduction

COVID-19 has changed our lives in ways we never imagined. The COVID-19 pandemic has forced global lifestyle changes. It changed lives both big and small.

Many companies lost international and domestic sales due to the pandemic and lockdown. Such dealings cost them a lot. China's manufacturing decline disrupted global supply chains. China makes IBM and Apple, among other IT leaders. iPhone

A. A. Zaveri (✉) · J. Jaafar
Malaysian Institute of Information Technology, Universiti Kuala Lumpur, Kuala Lumpur, Malaysia
e-mail: zaveri.ayesha@s.unikl.edu.my

J. Jaafar
e-mail: jjuliana@unikl.edu.my

E. Yafi
Faculty of Engineering and Information Technology, University of Technology Sydney, Sydney, New South Wales, Australia
e-mail: eiad.yafi@uts.edu.au

A. Ismail et al. (eds.), *Emerging Technologies and Sustainable Solutions*, SpringerBriefs in Applied Sciences and Technology,
https://doi.org/10.1007/978-3-032-18181-7_10

shortages have cost Apple 70% of its shares. Many technology conferences, events, and gatherings were canceled, costing sponsors and financiers US$1 billion. New startups and businesses benefited from such events and meetings. Big companies showcase their products and services, but the cancelation of such proceedings has affected IT market opportunities [1, 2]. This pandemic has exacerbated and affected global industries, sectors, and companies. However, IT companies worldwide have reported a sharp increase in demand for tech professionals [3].

In 2020, most IT projects were delayed or canceled, which slowed IT sector growth. In the first quarter of 2020, IT service providers saw a 4% drop in profits from hardware sales. They are working hard to recover in the coming quarters. IT industry opportunities and threats include the growing need for 5G technology. It will improve remote communications connections. Many companies and organizations prioritize this due to the pandemic. Telehealth is a growing sector. It enabled remote diagnosis, treatment, and surgery. Many quarantined patients were helped by various apps [4].

IT has powered the economy during the COVID-19 lockdown. Due to more cases and restrictions, employees worked remotely. Software can be managed remotely thanks to offshore and outsourced development. To create new applications for the organization, agile has moved from face-to-face to virtual meetings. The core of companies—where innovation and creativity begin—has been stifled by limited shared workspaces. Agile software development project updates, standup meetings, consultations, brainstorming meetings, and sessions often occur informally but follow social distancing. Programmers who brainstormed and discussed ideas with colleagues during software development must adapt to remote working [5].

Developers worked remotely because they faced new challenges every day. They can collaborate via Zoom or other video-conferencing tools. Agile meetings and standups can still be done using video-conferencing tools to share screens. Modern interactive and communicative technology is useless. Low-code and no-code tools are cloud services, enabling remote development teams to innovate and collaborate [6]. Digital businesses and productions can now make millions of dollars with strategic and rational use. Unfortunately, those profits can be outshone by the millions they lose when their system is not properly planned, designed, and managed to meet clients' needs. Software development life cycle (SDLC) was created to overcome the fear of unsatisfied customers and unstructured applications. Many software development teams have used this theory. It began in the late 1960s to structure and standardize software development [7].

The pandemic has harmed software developers, engineers, designers, project managers, software requirement engineers, and other stakeholders in software development, comfort, efficiency, output, creativity, and productivity. Productivity and comfort are linked. Disaster awareness, pandemic anxiety, and home office ergonomics affect comfort and productivity. It also impacts the software development life cycle [8].

Vanson Bourne's January 2021 survey of 400 IT decision-makers found that technology can be strategically used to rebuild and reconfigure businesses during the COVID-19 pandemic. The majority agrees. It puts software development skills at the forefront of corporate development, enabling the creation of new line-of-business applications and the rewriting of old software-encoded processes to adapt to rapid public policy changes [9].

10.2 Background Literature

The COVID-19 impressions have tested companies' and organizations' capacity and ability to deliver software applications or products efficiently and successfully. Some organizations quickly adopted the change, with the team members and other stakeholders involved in remote working and virtual environments, while some failed to adjust to the new norms. As organizations and companies strive hard to start to turn their faces to a new normal, it is a must that the processes and steps involved in the development of the products or software applications will adjust and variate according to the unique unfavorable situation and how the software development life cycle will endure the new usual [10]. The rapid and large-scale shift to working remotely disrupted ongoing projects and programs, forcing abrupt changes to project management. This often-required resetting delivery processes, with some projects needing major changes to stay effective. Thus, collaboration and governance drive the differentiation of adaptation effort in programs phases [11]. In the software development life cycle, functional code produced, tested, secured, managed, deployed, maintained, and put into live production is the most important metric. Is video conferencing and messaging more productive for engineers than face-to-face meetings? How it affected software development [12]

The software development life cycle is a systematic method for creating high-quality, cost-effective software. SDLC entails planning, analysis, design, development, testing, and deployment. It describes how to create, maintain, modify, and upgrade software. It can be utilized by system experts, business analysts, software engineers, designers, developers, and programmers to plan and implement systems or applications in a timely and cost-effective manner [13]. The SDLC enables IT firms to rapidly transform complex systems into more explicit and reliable products. The software life cycle improves software quality and development. Each stage generates results for the next. The design reflects requirements. Developers then code and build the software from design specifications and details. Quality control engineers use various methods to validate and test software. Product deployment follows testing [14, 15]. Over time, more characteristics and new models are added to this SDLC theory to modernize its framework in accordance with the evolving needs of producers and consumers [16]. This world is occasionally confronted with numerous unfavorable situations, such as the COVID-19 pandemic, and as a result, the user's needs fluctuate. SDLC must, therefore, strategically adapt to the changes.

10.3 Impact of COVID-19 on Software Engineering

The software engineering cycle globally experienced two major shifts: Working remotely and buying and selling online. Market–customer digital interaction become smooth and contagious. Digital marketing grew unexpectedly. Companies had to adapt to the rapidly changing online trading market. Software dominates most companies' strategies in this digital age. Well-prepared companies handled these unfavorable conditions well and caught up in the race. Instead of these crises, the new modernized and amended software engineering processes can improve functioning competencies and decision-making. Redesigning of software engineering processes can be done as follows (Fig. 10.1):

- Embracing new coding methods to improve software development to be more adaptable, flexible, and automated. Companies should priorities customer satisfaction and results over emerging requirements.
- Grasp the technologies and processes that triggered this transition and promote a clear and preemptive culture of identifying and addressing client requirements before they are said or otherwise exposed.
- Developing a data-driven system. Data-extraction digitalization tools are in high demand. Advanced data management skills must be valued and recruited. To meet end-user needs, data management requires new infrastructure, tools, methods, policies, and rules. Tools like these will give the Internet of Things and AI more space in technology, laying the groundwork for companies to thrive with new technology. In the COVID-19 pandemic, data digitization was the main global asset.
- Centering digital structure on the cloud. After COVID-19, cloud approaches must balance cost savings, investments, and organizational versatility by revealing innovation on a scale to meet top- and bottom-line business needs in these challenging times. Addressing software engineering organizations' longstanding obstacles is

Fig. 10.1 Post-COVID amendments in software engineering

necessary. To optimize and streamline applications, companies should migrate to the cloud professionally and technically. After analysis, clients moving their work to the cloud will help businesses enter the cloud. It will help companies improve their workflow and cloud resource availability.

- Modernizing collaboration and communication with virtual pods. Collaborations and meetings follow the remote world and work. Software development uses pods. Virtual pods feel like sitting next to people. According to the analysis, 88% of members agreed that pod-based software engineering is the only way.
- Understanding human nature and its needs in the digital age. As human needs change, monitoring, understanding, interpreting, and implementing them is the most difficult and critical process. Software developers can do it if they collaborate with project owners and users.
- Cultivating a culture to empower the digitalized and computerized future. A culture that understands and complements advanced reality needs to switch to a computerized show [17, 18].

10.4 Impact of COVID-19 on Software Development Life Cycle

The spread of the COVID-19 pandemic has had a substantial influence on SDLC in countries all over the world. The following is a list of some of how COVID-19 has impacted the various stages of the SDLC process:

Planning and Requirements Gathering: The pandemic has caused market uncertainty, affecting project timelines and budgets. This has forced firms to reassess their priorities, delaying planning, and requirement collection. Due to unfavorable conditions, upcoming software application requirements are difficult and complex. The software development life cycle must adapt to users' rapidly changing needs.

Design and Development: The pandemic has forced several software development teams to work remotely. Collaboration and communication issues may affect design and development. To improve communication and collaboration, remote teams must adopt new methods, technologies, and procedures.

Testing: Testing hardware and providing real-time feedback has become more complicated as more people work remotely. Due to remote labor issues, many companies have had to adjust their testing procedures.

Deployment: The epidemic has created delays in deployment due to changes in project timeframes and budgets. The pandemic has induced these delays. Remote work has made team deployments harder to organize, increasing deployment time.

Maintenance: Working remotely has made it harder to find and fix flaws during the pandemic. This has increased maintenance request response times.

COVID-19 has greatly affected software development. Project timeframes, budgets, and remote work drive this impact [19–21].

10.5 Reconstructing Software Engineering Process

Businesses must change their software development strategies to accommodate these changes. To adapt to changing consumer habits, companies must rethink software development. Many potential architectures, design patterns, technologies, infrastructure configurations, and development strategies exist. However, to create long-lasting, adaptable software, the following strategic imperatives must be met:

1. ***A well-coordinated business and software development plan.***

The epidemic has shown how important software is to modern businesses in all sectors. Developing software tailored to its users' demands is the goal.

When reevaluating the software approach, businesses should keep a few things in mind: whether the software or application allows the users to transact whenever and wherever the user requires; whether the application has access to the appropriate interaction methods (web browser, mobile app, voice)?; and whether the interface is so user-friendly that minimal instruction is required for the user to navigate. In summary, the software or application provided to the user is entirety productive and pleasant.

2. ***A cloud-based plan that is solid, safe, and extensible.***

Most businesses are already preparing for cloud migration. Maximizing cloud benefits is the question. It is essential to ask whether the created apps can maximize the cloud's scalability, automation, and flexibility. To answer yes, enterprises need a cloud-friendly or cloud-native application architecture. To answer no, they must lift and shift monolithic apps to the cloud.

Businesses must also assess application safety. Cloud-native deployments are dispersed and hard to manage. They need a comprehensive security strategy that includes web application firewalls and advanced runtime application self-protection.

3. ***An efficient, modern, and advanced approach to development.***

Accept DevOps now. Agile and DevOps can push working code to production faster than waterfall development. Software engineers and designers should also be located. Co-location has replaced in-sourcing, outsourcing, and offshoring. Programmers need remote work due to the COVID-19 pandemic. Teams need IDEAs like Visual Studio Code, Eclipse, NetBeans; pair-programming tools like Slack and Miro; and teleconferencing apps like Webex and GoToMeeting (USE Together, Visual Studio Live Share).

4. ***Transforming while performing***

As COVID-19 subsides, successful companies will follow these guidelines. Studies suggest companies start now by:

- Digitization and supply chain modernization. Businesses need digital communication with customers and suppliers to quickly adapt to changing market conditions. These channels must be equally accessible to internal and external users.
- Services are moving to the cloud for its scalability, automation, and adaptability. Businesses shouldn't settle for cloud app migration's limited benefits.
- Refactoring monolithic code into microservices modernizes legacy applications and reduces response time to changing user needs.
- Businesses should focus on application security rather than network perimeter security.
- Reaching out to people worldwide to work for a company is called "outsourcing," It may be done in several ways [22, 23].

10.6 Conclusion

COVID-19 has impacted software development. Due to the epidemic, many teams work remotely, requiring more agile development methods and tools. Automation, virtualization, and cloud-based solutions are gaining popularity due to the need for faster development. Protecting remote teams' data has increased the need for more secure and trustworthy software. Software engineering has felt the economic impact of the pandemic. Businesses have had to reallocate funds to meet new challenges while maintaining strict software safety and dependability standards. Thus, open-source software is promoted [22]. Finally, the pandemic has affected software collaboration. Remote teams require more collaboration and communication software. Remote teams are now responsible for making their product available to all users, increasing the need for diverse and inclusive teams [23].

Acknowledgements University support for this research is acknowledged.

References

1. R. Colomo-Palacios, A. Hernández-López, A. García-Crespo, P. Soto-Acosta, A Study of emotions in requirements engineering, in *Organizational, Business, and Technological Aspects of the Knowledge Society. WSKS 2010. Communications in Computer and Information Science*, vol. 112, ed. by M.D. Lytras, P. Ordonez de Pablos, P. Ziderman, A. Roulstone, A. Maurer, J.B. Imber (Springer, Berlin, Heidelberg, 2010)
2. A. Sutcliffe, Emotional requirements engineering, in *2011 IEEE 19th International Requirements Engineering Conference, Trento, Italy* (2011), pp. 321–322
3. K. Billie, *The State of Agile Project Management in 2020 and The Covid-19 Impact* (2020). https://www.invensislearning.com/blog/agile-project-management-in-2020/. Accessed 20th October 2022

4. S. Allen, *Software Engineering Takes on New Meaning in the Covid-19 Pandemic* (2020). https://cse.umn.edu/msse/news/software-engineering-takes-new-meaning-covid-19-pandemic. Accessed 26th May 2020
5. K. Thomas, *Agile Software Development Teams During and after Covid-19* (2020). https://knowledge.essec.edu/en/innovation/agile-software-development-during-after-COVID19.html. Accessed 15th May 2020
6. P. Ralph, S. Baltes, G. Adisaputri, R. Torkar, V. Kovalenko, M. Kalinowski, N. Novielli, S. Yoo, X. Devroey, X. Tan, M. Zhou, B. Turhan, R. Hoda, H. Hata, G. Robles, A. Milani Fard, R. Alkadhi, Pandemic programming: how COVID-19 affects software developers and how their organizations can help. Empir. Softw. Eng. **25**(6), 4927–4961 (2020)
7. O. de Weck, D. Krob, L. Lefei, P.C. Lui, A. Rauzy, X. Zhang, Handling the COVID-19 crisis: towards an agile model-based systems approach. Syst. Eng. **23**, 656–670 (2020)
8. L. Bao, T. Li, X. Xia et al., How does working from home affect developer productivity?—a case study of Baidu during the COVID-19 pandemic. Sci. China Inf. Sci. **65**, 142102 (2022)
9. E. Jackson, *Design of a Remote Emotional Requirements Elicitation Feedback Method* (2020). https://doi.org/10.13140/RG.2.2.31114
10. D. Batra, The impact of the COVID-19 on organizational and information systems agility. Inf. Syst. Manag. **37**(4), 361–365 (2020)
11. L. Khai, *Software Development Life Cycle* (2020). https://medium.com/dwarves-foundation/software-development-life-cycle-101-15ae4641321c. Accessed 1 Sep 2020
12. P. Neto, U.A. Mannan, E. Almeida, N. Nagappan, L.O. David, P.S. Kochhar, C. Gao, I. Ahmed, A deep dive into the impact of COVID-19 on software development. IEEE Trans. Softw. Eng. **48**(9), 3342–3360 (2022)
13. C. Albert, *Mastering The Remote Software Development Process During COVID* (2020). https://www.techzone360.com/topics/techzone/articles/2020/09/03/446460-mastering-remote-software-development-process-during-covid-19.htm. Accessed 3 Sept 2020
14. S. Kute, S. Thorat, *A Review of Various Software Development Life Cycle (SDLC) Models* (2014)
15. Z. Subhan, A. Bhatti, Requirements analysis and design in the context of various software development approaches. Int. J. Res. Appl. Sci. Eng. **3** (2015)
16. S. Shylesh, *A Study of Software Development Life Cycle Process Models. SSRN* (2017)
17. ByDrec, *Problems to Avoid During System Development Life Cycle* (2020). https://blog.bydrec.com/problems-system-development-life-cycle. Accessed 20 May 2020
18. ByDrec, *SDLC Pitfalls and How to Prevent Them* (2020). https://blog.bydrec.com/top-7-sdlc-pitfalls-and-how-to-prevent-them. Accessed 20 June 2020
19. V. Rastogi, *Software Development Life Cycle Models-Comparison, Consequences* (2014)
20. H. Douglas, *Comparing Traditional Systems Analysis and Design with Agile Methodologies* (2009). https://www.umsl.edu/~hugheyd/is6840/waterfall.html. Accessed September 2009
21. G. Gurung, R. Shah, D. Jaiswal, Software development life cycle models-a comparative study. Int. J. Sci. Res. Comput. Sci. Eng. Inform. Technol. 30–37 (2020). https://doi.org/10.32628/CSEIT206410
22. R. Paul, B. Sebastian, A.·Gianisa, T. Richard, K. Vladimir, K. Marcos, N. Nicole, Y. Shin, D. Xavier, T. Xin, Z. Minghui, T. Burak, H. Rashina, H. Hideaki, R. Gregorio, F. Amin Milani, A. Rana, Pandemic programming How COVID-19 affects software developers and how their organizations can help. Empiric. Softw. Eng. **25**, 4927–4961, Springer (2020)
23. A. Haroon, A. Sattam, I.B. Safa'a, COVID-19 and software development. IJCSNS Int. J. Comput. Sci. Netw. Secur. **22**(10), 359 (2022)

Chapter 11
Generative Adversarial Network Driver View Image Synthesis for Autonomous Vehicle Training

Athanasius Joseph, Adizul Ahmad, Ihsan Mohd Yassin, Azlee Zabidi, Rajeswari Raju, and Megat Syahirul Amin Megat Ali

Abstract Autonomous vehicles (AVs) are emerging due to their potential to reduce human error in transportation. Essential to AVs are subsystems for navigation and safety, including lane detection, often utilizing AI to analyze camera-captured images. AI performance hinges on training data quality and quantity, which may be lacking in atypical driving scenarios. To address this, we explore the use of generative adversarial networks (GANs) for generating realistic training data. GANs employ two networks, a generator and a discriminator, in a mutually challenging training process. Our study uses driver-view images to train a MATLAB-based GAN, which successfully generates diverse, realistic images, as demonstrated by our tests.

A. Joseph
Precious Credence Sdn. Bhd., Kuching, Malaysia
e-mail: athanjoe96@gmail.com

A. Ahmad
College of Engineering, Universiti Teknologi MARA, Shah Alam, Malaysia
e-mail: adizul@uitm.edu.my

I. M. Yassin (✉) · M. S. A. M. Ali
Microwave Research Institute, Universiti Teknologi MARA, Shah Alam, Malaysia
e-mail: ihsan_yassin@uitm.edu.my

M. S. A. M. Ali
e-mail: megatsyahirul@uitm.edu.my

A. Zabidi
Faculty of Systems and Software Engineering, College of Computing and Applied Sciences, Universiti Malaysia Pahang, Pekan, Malaysia
e-mail: azlee@ump.edu.my

R. Raju
School of Computing and Mathematics, Universiti Teknologi MARA, Kuala Terengganu, Malaysia
e-mail: rajes332@uitm.edu.my

A. Ismail et al. (eds.), *Emerging Technologies and Sustainable Solutions*, SpringerBriefs in Applied Sciences and Technology,
https://doi.org/10.1007/978-3-032-18181-7_11

Keywords Generative adversarial network · Autonomous vehicle · Computer vision · Data synthesis

11.1 Introduction

An autonomous vehicle (AV) operates independently using sophisticated sensors to navigate and steer, relying heavily on machine learning (ML) to adapt to diverse driving environments [1]. AV technology, attracting significant industry interest, promises reduced accidents and traffic congestion [1]. However, AV systems must adapt to multi-modal, dynamic settings and unseen scenarios, demanding extensive learning from both typical and atypical traffic conditions [2, 3]. Key challenges in AV development include lane detection accuracy, object recognition, and distance estimation, necessitating robust ML models trained on diverse data [4, 5]. However, acquiring sufficient real-world data, especially for rare scenarios, is difficult. Here, GANs emerge as a solution, generating realistic, diverse training data without significant deviation from real-world data [4, 6]. GANs involve two networks, a generator and a discriminator, improving iteratively through a game theory-based approach.

Our study utilized driver-view images to train a MATLAB-based GAN, aiming to synthesize images for ML training in object detection and lane curvature estimation. We detail our training process on dual graphics processing units (GPUs), demonstrating the GAN's efficacy in generating usable data for AV system development.

Research in AV emphasizes safety, with GANs playing a crucial role in simulating complex real-world scenarios. For instance, [6] developed a customized GAN to synthesize pedestrian behaviors, enhancing AV training. This "Ped-Cross GAN" generated sequences using a modified Wasserstein loss function to stabilize training. Similarly, [7] introduced a continuous conditional GAN (CCGAN) for creating diverse road images influenced by steering angles, employing an improved label input technique for enhanced performance. Further advancements include social GAN-based network [8], predicting vehicle trajectories using data from YOLO v3 and SORT algorithms. This SGAN outperformed traditional LSTM networks in trajectory prediction. Works by [9] presented a generative model combining feature extraction network (FEN) and path generation network (PGN) for pathway generation in autonomous driving, showcasing superior performance on the ETRI-Driving dataset. Reference [10] explored pedestrian trajectory simulation using a conditional speed GAN (CSG), offering effective data augmentation in varied scenarios. Addressing privacy concerns, [11] developed ADGAN models to anonymize sensitive data in AV-captured images and videos. For path planning, [12] proposed a CGAN with modified RRT algorithm (CGANRRT*) to optimize pathfinding in complex environments. Video prediction for vehicle movements was advanced by [13] through a video prediction GAN (VPGAN), incorporating adversarial inference and cycle-consistent loss functions. Similarly, [14] utilized a spatio-temporally coupled GAN (STC-GAN) for predictive scene parsing, merging CNN and LSTM architectures for enhanced spatial and semantic understanding. Works by [3] used dynamic Bayesian networks for AV anomaly detection, combining GANs with probabilistic switching models. [4]'s conditional GAN framework focused on visual attention in driving scenarios, creating saliency heatmaps for dynamic object focusing. Patil et al. [5]'s study on speed bump detection for electric vehicles employed a conditional GAN, proving its efficacy even with limited training data. Interestingly, [15] research utilized enhanced super-resolution GANs (ESRGAN) to improve data trustworthiness among networked AVs. Lastly, [2] demonstrated GAN's utility in simulating rare traffic conditions, using a cycle GAN-based network to augment vision-based perception modules in AVs.

11.2 Methodology

The research method is summarized in four main steps. The study employed the Point Gray Blackfly Camera BFLY-U3-23S6C-C, featuring a Sony IMX249 Progressive Scan CMOS sensor. This sensor captures images at 1920 × 1200 resolution at 41 FPS. The camera, mounted on the car's roof at an 8-degree pitch and a height of approximately 1.4 m, required calibration for accurate data acquisition. Calibration involved using a 6 × 8-inch checkerboard. The process entailed moving and tilting the checkerboard in various orientations, while the camera captured these variations. MATLAB calibration software then processed these images, detecting the checkerboard edges to determine the optimal camera settings. The settings were tested by re-projecting the detection results onto the original images, with reprojection error measurements confirming calibration accuracy.

Photographs for the study were captured during sunny daytime conditions in Puncak Alam and Meru, Malaysia, using a frame rate of approximately 30 FPS. This process yielded 10,000 JPEG images. For training preparation, these images were organized into a dedicated folder by class and image type. After an initial filtering process, the final dataset comprised 8386 images. Additionally, folder paths were established to enable the code to access the original images for synthesizing new ones.

GAN training involves the interplay between two networks: the discriminator and the generator, both refined using backpropagation algorithms. The generator aims to create images deceptive enough to fool the discriminator, while the discriminator strives to differentiate real from synthetic images. This competition enhances their performance until the discriminator can't distinguish synthetic images from real ones. The discriminator network comprises various layers. It starts with an input layer for 64 × 64 × 3 sized images, followed by a dropout layer (set at a probability of 0.5) to prevent overfitting. Convolution layers extract key features and edges, using progressively larger filters. Batch normalization aids in stabilizing training, while the leaky rectified linear units (ReLUs) layer adds non-linearity. The generator is crucial for synthesizing data. It starts with a project and reshape layer, transforming the input noise into a $4 \times 4 \times 512$ matrix. Transposed convolution layers reverse the discriminator's convolution process, initially using 5×5 filters. This is complemented by ReLU and batch normalization layers for non-linearity and training efficiency.

Training parameters included a minibatch size of 128 and 32,500 epochs, with minibatch size adjusted based on GPU memory constraints and epochs determined through trial and error for optimal results. Throughout training, the discriminator evaluates synthetic images from the generator, with penalties applied to the generator for any correctly identified fakes.

11.3 Results and Discussion

Our GAN was trained using two different GPUs: the NVidia GeForce 820 m and the NVidia GeForce RTX 2060. The training completion times were starkly different: 270 h on the 820 m and just 3 h on the RTX 2060, as shown in Fig. 11.1. This significant time difference is attributed to the RTX 2060's superior hardware, boasting 1920 CUDA cores and 6 GB of GPU memory, compared to the 820 m's 96 cores and 2 GB memory. The larger number of CUDA cores in the RTX 2060 greatly expedited the computation of network weights during training. The 820 m's limitations led to extended training time and challenges in allocating minibatch memory. Despite the disparities in training duration, the image quality generated by both GPUs was comparably high. Figure 11.2 depicts the optimal curves for the generator and discriminator, illustrating a good training balance: the discriminator's fitness function approached 1, while the generator's approached 0, indicating the generator's success in producing images nearly indistinguishable from real ones.

In training the GAN, maintaining a balance between the generator and discriminator networks was crucial. Both networks needed to improve consistently to effectively synthesize and discriminate images.

An imbalance, where one network outperforms the other, could lead to training failure. Two types of convergence failures are notable: discriminator dominance, where the generator fails to fool the discriminator, and generator dominance, often seen in early training phases. Our GAN avoided these issues, as evidenced by balanced training progress shown in Fig. 11.3. The divergent curves of the discriminator and generator indicated a healthy training process without dominance by either network. The quality of images produced by the generator correlated with the number of training epochs. With a higher number of epochs, the GAN had more opportunities to refine its weights, leading to improved image quality. This progression is visible in Fig. 11.3. At 500 epochs, images were blurry and pixelated, improving at 4000 epochs, and reaching near-realistic quality at 32,500 epochs. Thus, increasing epochs positively influenced the quality of synthesized datasets. Additionally, we observed no mode collapse, a condition where the generator produces repetitive images. The diversity in synthesized images across different epochs indicated a successful avoidance of mode collapse.

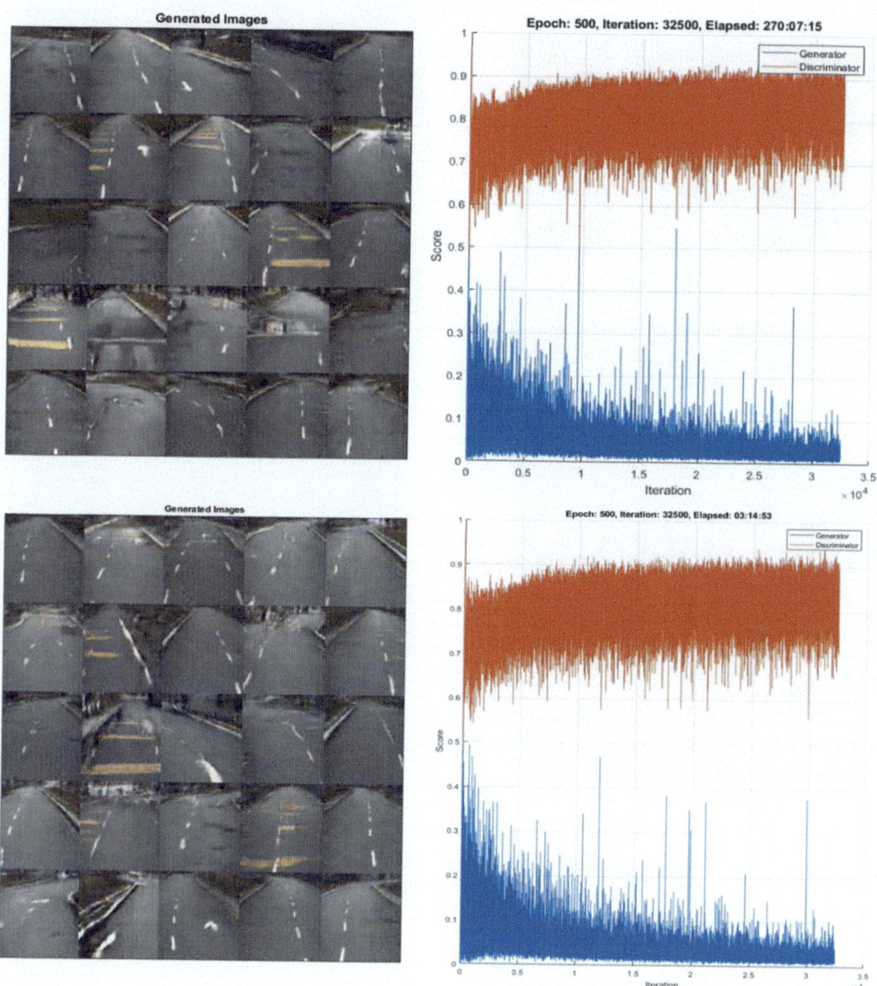

Fig. 11.1 Generated images and training plot on NVidia GeForce 820 m (row 1), and NVidia GeForce RTX2060 (row 2)

11.4 Conclusion

A GAN to synthesize driver-view images of an AV has been described in the paper. The GAN's generator network successfully produced realistic images with sufficient diversity—indicating that training has been successful. The effect of CUDA cores and training epochs to the synthesized image quality has been described. The discovery, in this paper, has the potential to be further expanded to training robust ML systems with accurate object detection and navigation capabilities.

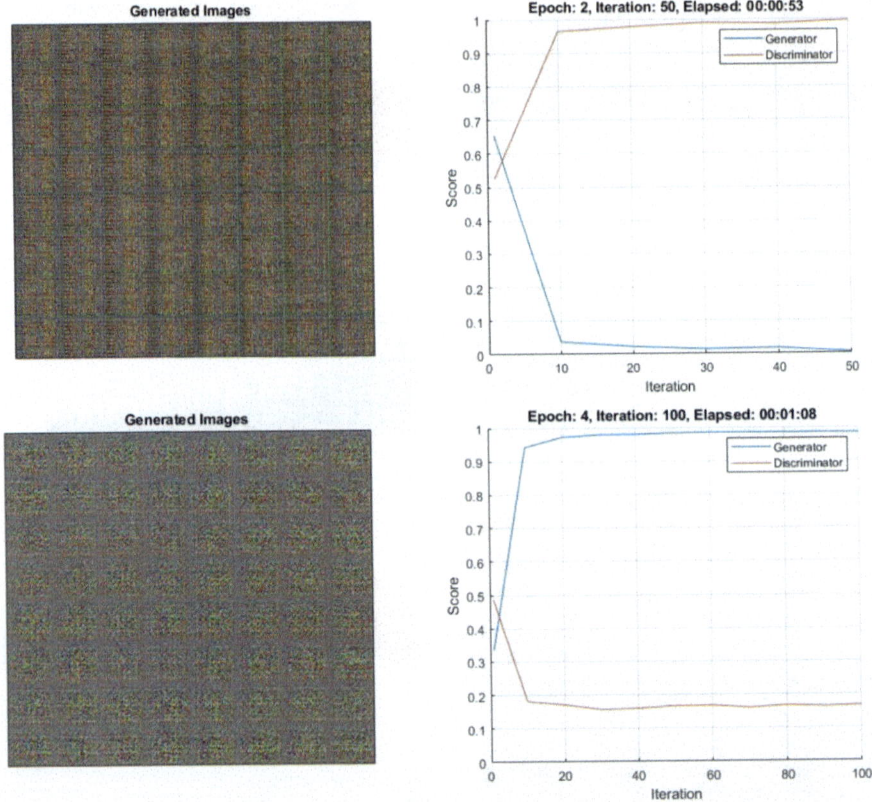

Fig. 11.2 Examples of discriminator (row 1) and generator (row 2) dominance

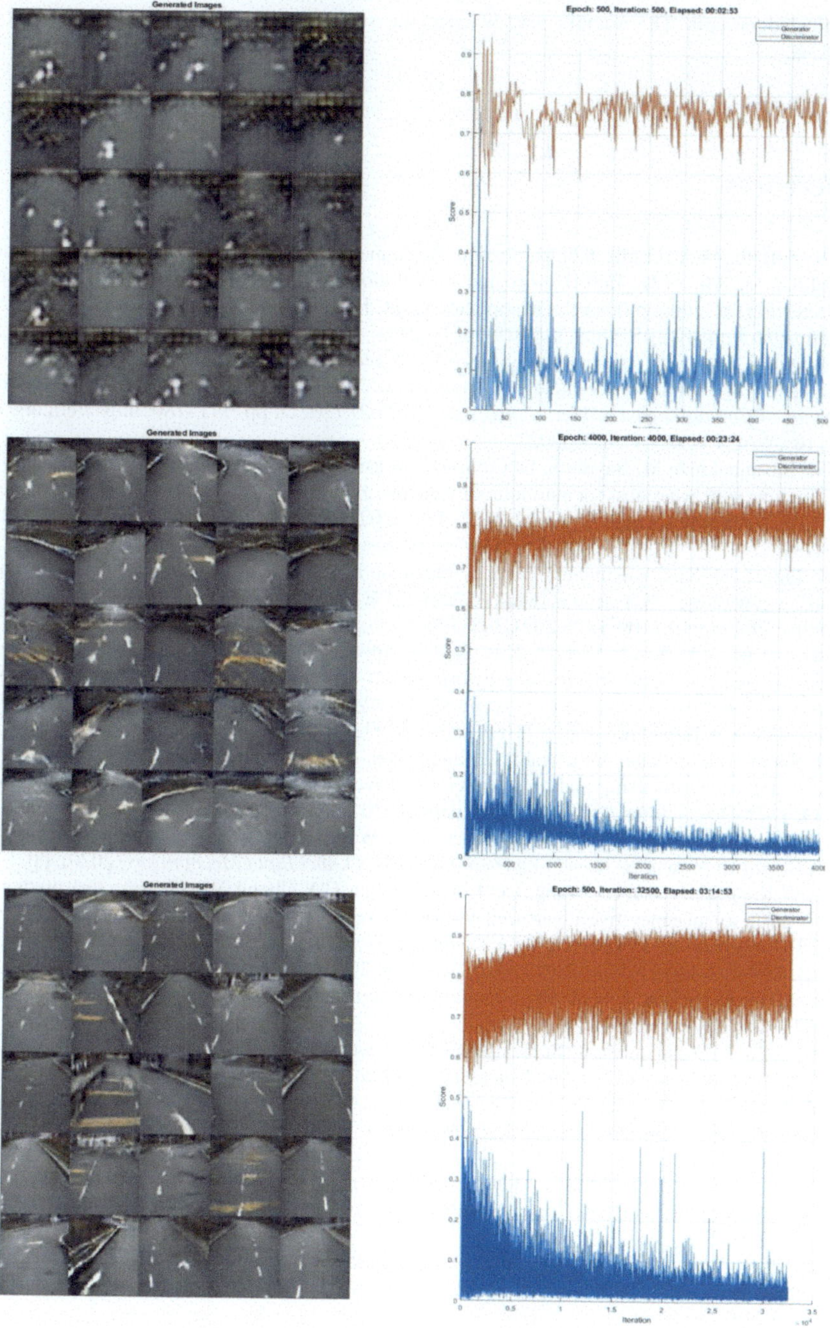

Fig. 11.3 Generator image quality at 500 (row 1), 4000 (row 2), and 32,500 (row 3) epochs

Acknowledgements The authors acknowledge the support by Universiti Teknologi MARA, Malaysia.

References

1. N. Zulkifli, M.A.I. Laili, S.N.M. Saadon, A. Ahmad, A. Zabidi, I.M. Yassin, F.H.K. Zaman, M.S.A.M. Ali, M.N. Taib, Fast region convolutional neural network lane and road defect detection for autonomous vehicle application. Int. J. Adv. Trends Comput. Sci. Eng. **8** (2019). https://doi.org/10.30534/ijatcse/2019/6681.32019
2. W. Xu, N. Souly, P.P. Brahma, Reliability of GAN generated data to train and validate perception systems for autonomous vehicles, in *Proceedings-2021 IEEE Winter Conference on Applications of Computer Vision Workshops, WACVW 2021* (2021), pp. 171–180. https://doi.org/10.1109/WACVW52041.2021.00023
3. M. Ravanbakhsh, M. Baydoun, D. Campo, P. Marin, D. Martin, L. Marcenaro, C. Regazzoni, Learning self-awareness for autonomous vehicles: exploring multisensory incremental models. IEEE Trans. Intell. Transp. Syst. **22**, 3372–3386 (2021). https://doi.org/10.1109/TITS.2020.2984735
4. F. Lateef, M. Kas, Y. Ruichek, Saliency heat-map as visual attention for autonomous driving using generative adversarial network (GAN). IEEE Trans. Intell. Transport. Syst. 1–14 (2021). https://doi.org/10.1109/TITS.2021.3053178
5. S.O. Patil, V.V. Sajith Variyar, K.P. Soman, Speed bump segmentation an application of conditional generative adversarial network for self-driving vehicles, in *Proceedings of the 4th International Conference on Computing Methodologies and Communication* (ICCMC 2020), pp. 935–939. https://doi.org/10.1109/ICCMC48092.2020.ICCMC-000173
6. J. Spooner, V. Palade, M. Cheah, S. Kanarachos, A. Daneshkhah, Generation of pedestrian crossing scenarios using ped-cross generative adversarial network. Appl. Sci. (Switzerland). **11**, 1–21 (2021). https://doi.org/10.3390/app11020471
7. X. Ding, Y. Wang, Z. Xu, W.J. Welch, Z.J. Wang, *Continuous Conditional Generative Adversarial Networks: Novel Empirical Losses and Label Input Mechanisms* (2020), pp. 1–49
8. L.W. Kang, C.C. Hsu, I.S. Wang, T.L. Liu, S. Y. Chen, C.Y. Chang, Vehicle trajectory prediction based on social generative adversarial network for self-driving car applications, in *Proceedings-2020 International Symposium on Computer, Consumer and Control, IS3C 2020* (2020), pp. 489–492. https://doi.org/10.1109/IS3C50286.2020.00133
9. D. Choi, S. Han, K. Min, J. Choi, *PathGAN: Local Path Planning with Attentive Generative Adversarial Networks* (2020)
10. S. Julka, V. Sowrirajan, J. Schloetterer, M. Granitzer, *Conditional Generative Adversarial Networks for Speed Control in Trajectory Simulation* (2021)
11. Z. Xiong, Z. Cai, Q. Han, A. Alrawais, W. Li, ADGAN: protect your location privacy in camera data of auto-driving vehicles. IEEE Trans. Industr. Inform. **17**, 6200–6210 (2021). https://doi.org/10.1109/TII.2020.3032352
12. N. Ma, J. Wang, J. Liu, M.Q.H. Meng, Conditional generative adversarial networks for optimal path planning. IEEE Trans. Cogn. Dev. Syst. **8920**, 1–10 (2021). https://doi.org/10.1109/TCDS.2021.3063273
13. Z. Hu, T. Turki, J.T.L. Wang, Generative adversarial networks for stochastic video prediction with action control. IEEE Access **8**, 63336–63348 (2020). https://doi.org/10.1109/ACCESS.2020.2982750
14. M. Qi, Y. Wang, A. Li, J. Luo, STC-GAN: spatio-temporally coupled generative adversarial networks for predictive scene parsing. IEEE Trans. Image Process. **29**, 5420–5430 (2020). https://doi.org/10.1109/TIP.2020.2983567

15. J. Guo, Q. Yang, S. Fu, R. Boyles, S. Turner, K. Clarke, Towards trustworthy perception information sharing on connected and autonomous vehicles, in *Proceedings-2020 International Conference on Connected and Autonomous Driving, MetroCAD 2020* (2020), pp. 85–90. https://doi.org/10.1109/MetroCAD48866.2020.00021

Chapter 12
Predictive Maintenance Using a Long Short-Term Memory Model for Industrial Applications

Raja Fazliza Raja Suleiman, Wan Rusyhuddeen Faizzal Wan Zainal Abidin, and Norzanah Md Said

Abstract The conventional preventive maintenance (PM) run on schedule in factories is costly due to unnecessary machine downtime during the execution. The deployment of predictive maintenance (PdM) inline with the fourth industrial revolution is more advantageous than preventive maintenance. PdM may reduce repairing breakdown cost and time, allowing maintenance to occur before failure happens. This paper compares the prediction performance of long short-term memory (LSTM) with other machine learning models from the literature for predictive maintenance using the AI41 2020 synthetic dataset of a milling machine. Results show that LSTM performs better than the two other methods in terms of accuracy and precision. For recall and F1-score, random forest performs slightly better than LSTM.

Keywords Predictive maintenance · Machine failure · LSTM · AI4I2020

R. F. Raja Suleiman (✉) · W. R. F. W. Z. Abidin · N. M. Said
Mechatronics Engineering Technology Section, Malaysia France Institute, Universiti Kuala Lumpur, Bangi, Selangor, Malaysia
e-mail: fazliza@unikl.edu.my

W. R. F. W. Z. Abidin
e-mail: rusyhuddeen@s.unikl.edu.my

N. M. Said
e-mail: norzanah@unikl.edu.my

R. F. Raja Suleiman · N. M. Said
UniKL Robotics and Industrial Automation Center, Malaysia France Institute, Universiti Kuala Lumpur, Bangi, Selangor, Malaysia

R. F. Raja Suleiman
Centre for Women Advancement and Leadership, Universiti Kuala Lumpur, Kuala Lumpur, Malaysia

A. Ismail et al. (eds.), *Emerging Technologies and Sustainable Solutions*, SpringerBriefs in Applied Sciences and Technology,
https://doi.org/10.1007/978-3-032-18181-7_12

12.1 Introduction

Predictive maintenance (PdM) is replacing preventive maintenance (PM) for machinery in most factory settings because of the fourth industrial revolution. PdM depends on large datasets fed to learning models yielding an accurate predictions of machinery breakdown [1–3]. Modern factories strive to automate many processes, leveraging industrial machines that perform various tasks traditionally done by humans. However, these machines, like all mechanical systems, experience wear and tear over time, which can lead to sub-optimal performance or even failure [4].

Predictive maintenance offers a solution to this challenge. PdM uses data-driven methodologies to predict when a machine will require maintenance, enabling a proactive approach rather than reactive fixes after a machine fails. This methodology is part of a wider field of research, encompassing various techniques and methods, each suitable for different situations and types of data [5–7].

Machine learning models predict positive or negative classes based on the training of the fed dataset. For predictive maintenance applications, a large data sample is essential to obtain high model accuracy. This paper compares the neural network model with classical supervised learning models. From the literature, it was found that the LSTM method adapts well to sequential data types [8, 9], while decision tree and random forest were found to show a promising prediction performance for PdM [10–12].

12.2 Methodology

12.2.1 *Synthetic Dataset of an Industrial Milling Machine*

In the scope of the presented work, the AI4I 2020 synthetic dataset of milling machines [13] is utilized, which consists of 10,000 samples with 14 features, including identifiers, machine operating parameters (such as air temperature, rotational speed), and five types of machine failures (tool wear, heat dissipation, power failure, overstrain, and random failure). The machine state is labeled as failure if at least one of the five failure parameters is true. Figure 12.1 shows a sample of the AI4I 2020 dataset. For the learning model training and testing, the ratio applied is 70:30.

12.2.2 *LSTM as Learning Model*

Long short-term memory [14] is extended from recurrent neural networks that update the long-term memory based on the previous output and the current input. The long-term memory cell denoted by c_t which holds information at time t is:

	A	B	C	D	E	F	G	H	I	J	K	L	M	N
1	UDI	Product ID	Type	Air temperature [K]	Process temperature [K]	Rotational speed [rpm]	Torque [Nm]	Tool wear [min]	Machine failure	TWF	HDF	PWF	OSF	RNF
2	1	M14860	M	298.1	308.6	1551	42.8	0	0	0	0	0	0	0
3	2	L47181	L	298.2	308.7	1408	46.3	3	0	0	0	0	0	0
4	3	L47182	L	298.1	308.5	1498	49.4	5	0	0	0	0	0	0
5	4	L47183	L	298.2	308.6	1433	39.5	7	0	0	0	0	0	0
6	5	L47184	L	298.2	308.7	1408	40	9	0	0	0	0	0	0
7	6	M14865	M	298.1	308.6	1425	41.9	11	0	0	0	0	0	0
8	7	L47186	L	298.1	308.6	1558	42.4	14	0	0	0	0	0	0
9	8	L47187	L	298.1	308.6	1527	40.2	16	0	0	0	0	0	0
10	9	M14868	M	298.3	308.7	1667	28.6	18	0	0	0	0	0	0
11	10	M14869	M	298.5	309	1741	28	21	0	0	0	0	0	0
12	11	H29424	H	298.4	308.9	1782	23.9	24	0	0	0	0	0	0
13	12	H29425	H	298.6	309.1	1423	44.3	29	0	0	0	0	0	0
14	13	M14872	M	298.6	309.1	1339	51.1	34	0	0	0	0	0	0
15	14	M14873	M	298.6	309.2	1742	30	37	0	0	0	0	0	0
16	15	L47194	L	298.6	309.2	2035	19.6	40	0	0	0	0	0	0
17	16	L47195	L	298.6	309.2	1542	48.4	42	0	0	0	0	0	0
18	17	M14876	M	298.6	309.2	1311	46.6	44	0	0	0	0	0	0
19	18	M14877	M	298.7	309.2	1410	45.6	47	0	0	0	0	0	0
20	19	H29432	H	298.8	309.2	1306	54.5	50	0	0	0	0	0	0
21	20	M14879	M	298.9	309.3	1632	32.5	55	0	0	0	0	0	0
22	21	H29434	H	298.9	309.3	1375	42.7	58	0	0	0	0	0	0
23	22	L47201	L	298.8	309.3	1450	44.8	63	0	0	0	0	0	0
24	23	M14882	M	298.9	309.3	1581	30.7	65	0	0	0	0	0	0
25	24	L47203	L	299	309.4	1758	25.7	68	0	0	0	0	0	0
26	25	M14884	M	299	309.4	1561	37.3	70	0	0	0	0	0	0
27	26	L47205	L	299	309.5	1861	23.3	73	0	0	0	0	0	0
28	27	L47206	L	299.1	309.5	1512	39	75	0	0	0	0	0	0

Fig. 12.1 Sample of the AI4I 2020 dataset. Columns include product number, air temperature, process temperature, rotational speed, torque, tool wear, and several machine failure indicators. Each row represents a different product with specific measurements and failure data. The table is organized with headers for each column, providing a structured overview of the operational parameters and outcomes

$$c_t = f_t \odot c_{t-1} + i_1 \odot g_t \tag{12.1}$$

where i and f are, respectively, the input gate and forget gate (open and close access to the memory) and g represents the cell candidate which add information to the memory cell c_t.. The output state (or hidden state) at time t is:

$$\boldsymbol{h}_t = o_t \odot \sigma_c(\boldsymbol{c}_t) \tag{12.2}$$

where o_t denotes the output gate that controls the access to the hidden state at time t and σ_c is the activation function, which by default is tanh: the hyperbolic tangent function. Meanwhile, all the gates that control access to the memory state are activated by specific functions such as the sigmoid function or the softmax function. In Sec. 12.4 of this paper, both of these functions are applied to LSTM for comparison purposes to choose the better model accuracy.

Table 12.1 Comparison of classification performances for predictive maintenance of industrial machine

Evaluation parameters	Supervised learning methods (%)		
	LSTM	Decision tree	Random forest
Accuracy	99.99	97.95	98.6
Recall	96.90	96.75	98.6
Precision	99.99	97.88	98.5
F1-score	98.00	97.91	98.4

12.2.3 Predictive Maintenance Performance Evaluation

The prediction or classification performances [15] of the machine condition whether it is functional (label 0: negative class) or failure (label 1: positive class) are evaluated via the following parameters:

$$\text{Accuracy} = \frac{TP + TN}{TP + TN + FP + FN} \tag{12.3}$$

$$\text{Recall (TPR)} = \frac{TP}{TP + FN} \tag{12.4}$$

$$\text{Precision} = \frac{TP}{TP + FP} \tag{12.5}$$

$$\text{F1 score} = \frac{2TP}{2TP + FP + FN} \tag{12.6}$$

where TP is true positive that signifies correct prediction of machine failure, TN is true negative, representing the correct prediction of machine functioning, FP is false positive, meaning that the learning model predicts machine failure, but the actual state is machine functioning (type 1 error). Lastly, FN is false negative, which indicates the model wrongly predicts that the machine is functioning, but the machine is actually failing (type 2 error). Thus, in this setting, it is important to have a compromise between high TP and low FN to ensure a good prediction of machine failure. Results of the tested model performances using Eqs. (12.3)–(12.6) are shown in Table 12.1.

12.3 Results and Discussion

The LSTM learning model (Eqs. (12.1)–(12.2)) is applied to the AI41 2020 predictive maintenance dataset with epochs set at 15, 35, and 50 to obtain the training and testing accuracy while monitoring overfitting. For the output gate activation function, sigmoid and softmax are deployed in order to choose the better function. Figures 12.2

and 12.3 show the LSTM model accuracy and loss for the three epochs, with different output gate activation functions (sigmoid and softmax). It can be seen that the sigmoid function yields a better learning model for LSTM than the softmax function as the curve reaches stability. Comparing the number of epochs in Fig. 12.2, epoch 35 presents overfitting.

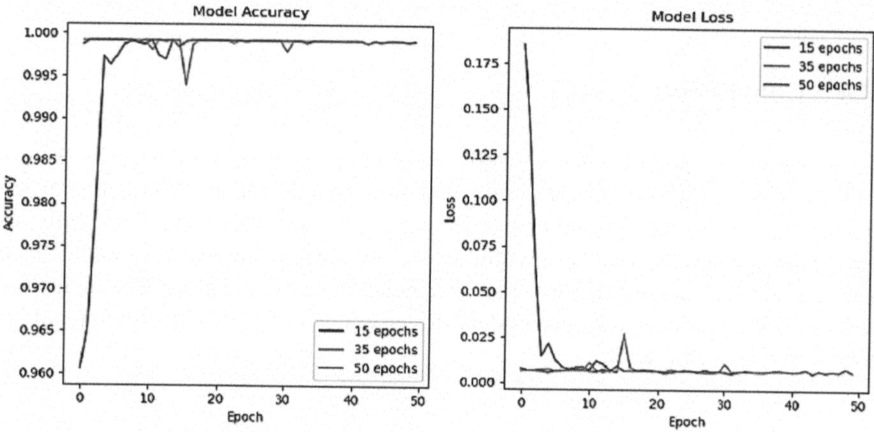

Fig. 12.2 The image consists of two X-Y charts comparing model performance of LSTM over different epochs with sigmoid output gate activation function. The left chart shows "Model Accuracy" with accuracy on the Y-axis and epochs on the X-axis. Three lines represent 15, 35, and 50 epochs, showing high accuracy across all epochs. The right chart displays "Model Loss" with loss on the Y-axis and epochs on the X-axis. The lines indicate a rapid decrease in loss initially, stabilizing at low values. A legend differentiates the lines by epoch count

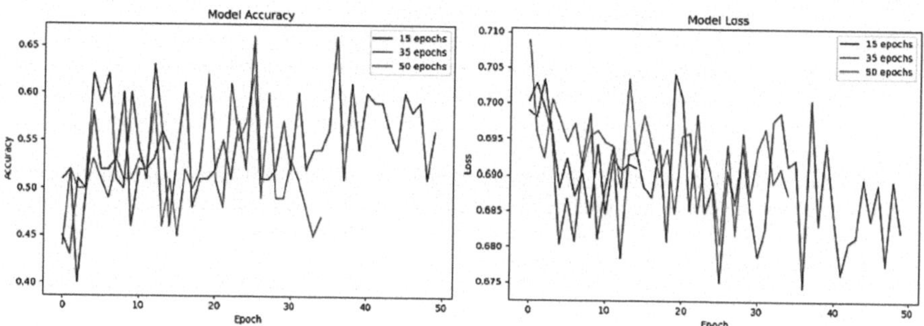

Fig. 12.3 The image consists of two X-Y charts for LSTM with softmax output gate activation function. The left chart shows "Model Accuracy" over 50 epochs, with three lines representing 15, 35, and 50 epochs in blue, red, and green, respectively. The right chart displays "Model Loss" over the same epochs, with the same color coding. The accuracy chart has a vertical axis labeled "Accuracy" ranging from 0.40 to 0.65, while the loss chart's vertical axis is labeled "Loss" ranging from 0.675 to 0.710. Both charts have a horizontal axis labeled "Epoch." The lines fluctuate, indicating variations in accuracy and loss across different epochs

On the other hand, the predictive maintenance LSTM model is compared to decision tree and random forest performances via Eqs. (12.3)–(12.6) as summarized in Table 12.1. Results show that LSTM performs better than the two other methods in terms of accuracy and precision. For recall and F1-score, the random forest performs slightly better than LSTM. The decision tree is the weaker model in the presented application.

12.4 Conclusion

The selection of a maintenance strategy is a critical decision, influenced by factors such as budget constraint, infrastructure, and the type of machinery. Predictive maintenance emerges as the optimal choice for high-value industries due to its ability to prevent unexpected machinery downtime. For future work, a predictive maintenance dataset with timestamps will allow the forecasting of machine failure. In conclusion, PdM is a better choice in the current data-driven era, which yields efficient operation and reduces cost and labor.

References

1. S. Arena, E. Florian, I. Zennaro, P.F. Orrù, F. Sgarbossa, A novel decision support system for managing predictive maintenance strategies based on machine learning approaches. Saf. Sci. **146**, 105529 (2022)
2. S. Vollert, M. Atzmueller, A. Theissler, Interpretable Machine Learning: A brief survey from the predictive maintenance perspective, in *2021 26th IEEE International Conference on Emerging Technologies and Factory Automation (ETFA)* (IEEE, 2021), pp. 01–08
3. P. Klein, N. Weingarz, R. Bergmann, Enhancing siamese neural networks through expert knowledge for predictive maintenance, in *IoT Streams for Data-Driven Predictive Maintenance and IoT, Edge, and Mobile for Embedded Machine Learning. ITEM IoT Streams 2020. Communications in Computer and Information Science*, ed. by J. Gama et al. vol. 1325 (Springer, Cham, 2020)
4. S. Kumar, S.K. Chandra, R.N. Shukla, L. Panigrahi, Industry 4.0 based machine learning models for anomalous product detection and classification, in *OPJU International Technology Conference on Emerging Technologies for Sustainable Development, OTCON 2022* (Institute of Electrical and Electronics Engineers Inc., 2022)
5. L.P. Silvestrin, M. Hoogendoorn, G. Koole, A comparative study of state-of-the-art machine learning algorithms for predictive maintenance, in *SSCI* (2019), pp. 760–767
6. T. Zonta, C.A. Da Costa, R. Da Rosa Righi, M.J. De Lima, E.S. Da Trindade G.P. Li, Predictive maintenance in The Industry 4.0: a systematic literature review. Comput. Industr. Eng. **150**, 106889 (2020)
7. Z.M. Çınar, N.A. Abdussalam, Q. Zeeshan, O. Korhan, M. Asmael, B. Safaei, Machine learning in predictive maintenance towards sustainable smart manufacturing in industry 4.0. Sustainability **12**(19), 8211 (2020)
8. R. Zhao, J. Wang, R. Yan, K. Mao, Machine Health Monitoring with LSTM networks, in *2016 10th international conference on sensing technology (ICST)* (IEEE, 2016), pp. 1–6
9. A. Graves, A. Graves, Long short-term memory, in *Supervised Sequence Labelling with Recurrent Neural Networks* (2012), pp. 37–45

10. S. Kaparthi, D. Bumblauskas, Designing predictive maintenance systems using decision tree-based machine learning techniques. Int. J. Qual. Reliabil. Manag. **37**(4), 659–686 (2020)
11. A. Ouadah, L. Zemmouchi-Ghomari, N. Salhi, Selecting an appropriate supervised machine learning algorithm for predictive maintenance. Int. J. Adv. Manufact. Technol. **119**(7–8), 4277–4301 (2022)
12. J.Y. Hsu, Y.F. Wang, K.C. Lin, M.Y. Chen, J.H.Y. Hsu, Wind turbine fault diagnosis and predictive maintenance through statistical process control and machine learning. IEEE Access **8**, 23427–23439 (2020)
13. S. Matzka, Explainable artificial intelligence for predictive maintenance applications, in *Third International Conference on Artificial Intelligence for Industries (AI4I)* (2020)
14. S. Hochreiter, J. Schmidhuber, Long short-term memory. Neural Comput. **9**(8), 1735–1780 (1997)
15. C. Sammut, G.I. Webb, *Encyclopedia of Machine Learning and Data Mining* (Springer Publishing Company, Incorporated, 2017)

Chapter 13
A Rule-Based Approach: Health Tracker for Inflammatory Bowel Disease Patients

Suriana Ismail, Nayli Umairah Azizan, Noor Widasuria Abu Bakar, Norhatta Mohd, and Husna Sarirah

Abstract Poor quality communication during consultation between patient and doctor tends to be a doctor-centered. Patients tend to give less information about their concerns to their doctors during the consultation process. The purpose of the research is to investigate the critical criteria of patients with inflammatory bowel disease (IBD) in relation to their appointment for health treatment. Gut Caretaker is a self-management mobile application that enables IBD patients to take control of their lifestyle better by adding their appointment dates and test results, and tracking their symptoms based on a rule-based approach. User evaluation on unit testing is conducted and shows a positive result.

Keywords Health tracker · Inflammatory bowel disease (IBD) · Patient · Mobile application · Symptom tracking

---

S. Ismail (✉) · N. U. Azizan · N. W. A. Bakar · N. Mohd
Malaysian Institute of Information Technology, Universiti Kuala Lumpur, Kuala Lumpur, Malaysia
e-mail: suriana@unikl.edu.my

N. U. Azizan
e-mail: nayli.azizan16@s.unikl.edu.my

N. W. A. Bakar
e-mail: widasuria@unikl.edu.my

N. Mohd
e-mail: norhatta@unikl.edu.my

H. Sarirah
Taylor's University, Subang Jaya, Selangor, Malaysia
e-mail: husna.husin@taylors.edu.my

A. Ismail et al. (eds.), *Emerging Technologies and Sustainable Solutions*, SpringerBriefs in Applied Sciences and Technology,
https://doi.org/10.1007/978-3-032-18181-7_13

13.1 Introduction

Every day, there are a lot of patients whom doctors need to attend public hospital specialist clinics. There could be a hundred patients daily. The need to handle a hundred patients may create a sense of urgency for doctors, leading to inefficient communication. An original article by UITM's academics, conducted for a four-week study, stated that the majority of patients (41.90%) spent between 11 and 20 min with the doctor, while 19.05% spent between 21 and 30 min [1]. This explains why a lot of other patients are waiting outside for a consultation with a doctor.

However, we cannot ask the doctor to treat the patient faster during the consultation as this could lead to miscommunication with the patient. One article titled "A Model of Doctor-Patient Communication and Information Seeking: A Study Among Trainee or Junior Doctors in Malaysian Hospitals" from UTM's academics stated that accurate patient health status information is crucial to make a diagnosis of a disease [2].

Besides, longer and slower consultations have advantages. It has been discovered that doctors who consult for less than 7 min are more prone to overlook patients' symptoms. Doctors are more likely to discover symptoms and carefully examine presenting complaints when they consult slowly and for a longer period.

Therefore, if there is a way to make the time each patient has with the doctor minimal, and at the same time we want them to have the best treatment and good communication about their treatment, it would be physical diaries. But apparently, physical diaries could easily be lost and are not stored in the hospital's database.

If there is an app that can ask patients basic questions a few days before their appointment day regarding their conditions and concerns, their sessions can be shorter without missing communication. By making a collaboration with Hospital Sungai Buloh, this system will be a great tool for the problem that patients and doctors face.

The following are problem statements:

i Patients record their health condition manually

There are patients who use physical books to easily track their symptoms. Even so, the book could be lost, as patients sometimes forget where they placed it. The years of tracking their symptoms can be wasted, although the doctor did summarize all the patient's symptoms in one sentence in the hospital [3].

ii. Poor-quality communication between doctor and patient on the appointment day

Some doctors did their consultations with patient faster because they worry about other patients waiting outside the room before closing time. Unfortunately, this can lead to poor-quality communication, as the consultation will be doctor-centered, and patients tend to give less information about their concerns to their doctors during the consultation process.

Thus, the objectives of the study are:

i. To analyze the problem of a patient's unorganized record for the doctor during an appointment.
ii. To develop a health-tracking mobile application based on a rule-based method.
iii. To evaluate the functionality of the Health Tracker Mobile Application by conducting system and user acceptance testing once it is fully developed.

Advantages of Native Mobile Applications

The benefits of developing native mobile applications are numerous. Speed is one of the main advantages. Native mobile apps are designed and compiled using the platform's core programming language and APIs, making them more efficient on this platform and having fewer device compatibility issues. Additionally, native mobile apps are compiled and stored on the mobile device to take full advantage of the device's processing power.

Apart from that, native mobile apps offer a more dynamic and intuitive user experience. Native mobile applications are more powerful than web applications. These native apps inherit the device's operating system interface, so they appear to be an integral part of the device. One of the most important advantages of native apps is that they provide an amazing user experience because they were designed specifically for the operating system. These applications enhance the user experience on the target operating system.

Additionally, native mobile applications are secure and reliable. Web applications are based on different browsers and technologies such as JavaScript, HTML5, and CSS, and their non-standard nature creates a large performance gap for web applications. Native apps, on the other hand, offer better security and performance.

Firebase

Firebase is a software development platform founded in 2011 and acquired by Google in 2014. The platform is a back-end solution as a service for mobile and web-based applications, including services for application development, testing, and management. A BaaS solution reduces the demands on back-end database management and associated infrastructure. The development of the application is using Flutter as it is a cross-platform tool for building Android and iOS apps from a single codebase using a modern reactive framework.

Figure 13.1 shows the architecture of Firebase. The 3-tier architectural style is a good way to describe how the Firebase database works. This need requires an intermediate management service to manage user profiles and a real-time database to store application and user data.

Health Monitoring

On a personal level, health monitoring refers to using technology to monitor a patient's health at home. Health care providers can monitor a person's condition remotely and call them only when needed.

Patients with IBD require constant monitoring of their disease and rapid adjustment of medical treatment regimens in the event of recurrence to improve clinical

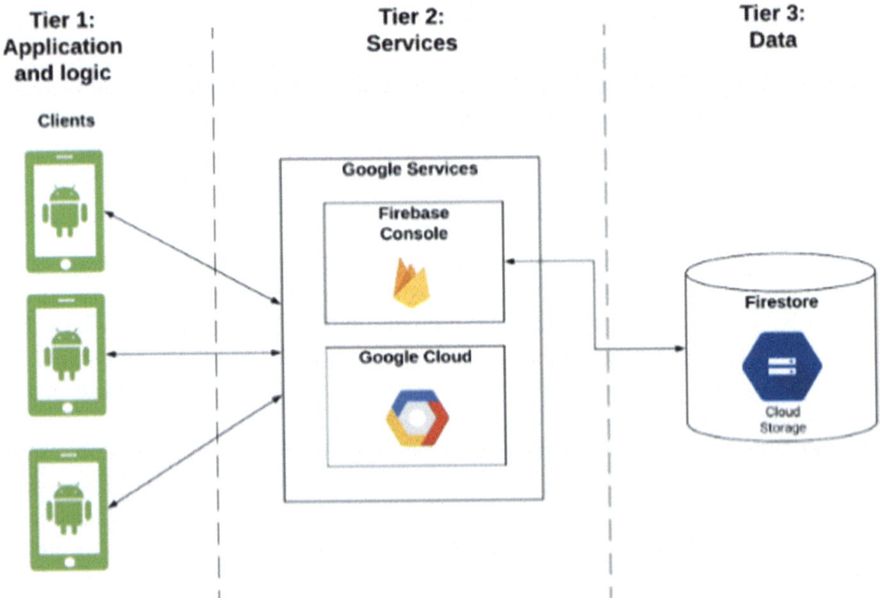

Fig. 13.1 System architecture

outcome and prevent further complications. It is also known that contact with health professionals involved in the management and monitoring of IBD may be important to better assess the real contribution of emotion to the disease state. This can reduce the number of disease recurrences [4].

Algorithm on Gut Caretaker's Symptom Score Feature

The Gut Caretaker application uses a rule-based method to assess how a patient feels about their condition as depicted in Fig. 13.2. They are asked to rate their health on a scale of zero to five on seven health-related topics. The application then calculates a final score by adding them together, which gives the patient how severe the symptoms are.

Using another system as comparison, a similar functionality is provided by Mood Tracker Pro. The app asks users a series of questions about how they feel, and based on their responses, it calculates the mode score.

The Gut Caretaker application and Mood Tracker Pro both benefit a lot from the symptom score features. By using numbers to give a picture of how they are doing, it helps patients gain a better knowledge of their health. Patient and doctor can communicate better when patients are aware of their symptom scores. Additionally, this feature in Gut Caretaker helps the doctor to identify patients who require additional care or attention.

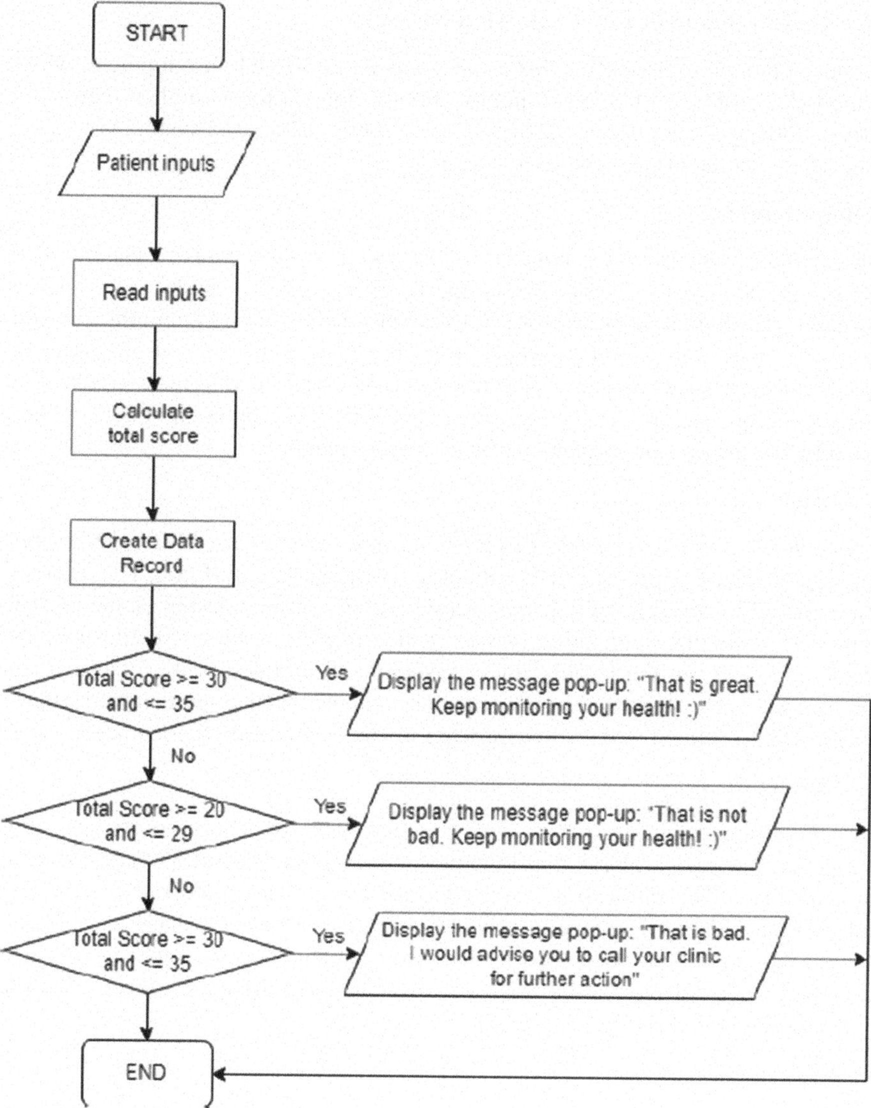

Fig. 13.2 System-based computation

13.2 Methodology

This section explains the methods, tools, and techniques used and the life cycle models of the application development of the research project. Prior to beginning the project, the primary objective is to obtain the relevant information.

Software Development Life Cycle Methodology

The development approach for this project was Agile Model Development, which ensured the building of a good-quality mobile application. Another reason for choosing this approach was its flexibility in accommodating ever-changing requirements based on the project end user's needs.

i. **Requirement**

In this phase, research was conducted on the unorganized records of patients with IBD during consultation with doctors and in their overall lifestyle. An interview was conducted with a nurse working at Hospital Sungai Buloh to gain insights into the gastro clinic. The project's scope was defined, focusing on both the user and the system. Consistent meetings with the supervisor were held to receive advice on the system requirements. This phase concluded with the completion of deliverables, including the project proposal and software requirements.

ii. **Design**

The second stage involved the development of a design for the Health Tracker Mobile App, specifically designed for IBD patients at Hospital Sungai Buloh. The information gathered in the early phase was translated into various design elements. The user interface of the application was created using FlutterFlow. To illustrate the interactions between the Health Tracker system and its users, a use case diagram was generated. The design of the user interface and the UML diagram adhered to the specifications outlined in the software requirements specification documents.

iii. **Development**

The development phase started with creating the application prototype after completing the design phase. Once the prototype was developed, it was connected to the database. The application's user interface was constructed using the Dart and Flutter programming language in FlutterFlow. The Firebase database was utilized to build the database, which sped up the development process. Each module was developed independently, and the app was evaluated in subsequent stages to ensure its proper functionality.

iv. **Testing**

During the development phase, the system underwent testing in real-world conditions to ensure its proper functioning. User acceptance testing was conducted to validate that the system development aligned with the initial user requirements. Representative users were involved to assess the application's usability and effectiveness.

Various testing techniques were implemented, including unit testing and system testing, to identify and resolve any potential issues. This approach aimed to meet all the defined requirements and ensure the overall reliability of the application.

v. **Deployment**

In this phase, the Gut Caretaker was made available to users. To ensure a smooth onboarding experience, an easy and streamlined installation process was implemented.

vi. **Review**

The Gut Caretaker mobile application's review phase was a continuous procedure aimed at problem solving and ongoing enhancement. Enhancements and upgrades were driven by user, stakeholder, and healthcare professional feedback. Smooth operation and consumer satisfaction were ensured by prompt issue resolution. Regular updates and releases introduced new features based on evolving needs. Maintenance includes security measures, software updates, and addressing technical issues. This iterative process ensured that the application for IBD patients and healthcare providers at Hospital Sungai Buloh continued to be efficient, user-friendly, and high quality.

13.3 Results and Discussion

Unit Testing

For the unit testing, each part of the Gut Caretaker application was tested against their functionality to ensure the accuracy of the modules. There are 24 test cases tested as described in Table 13.1, Use case description.

The results, as shown in Fig. 13.3, clearly show that the use cases tested are proven to meet all the requirements captured for the study.

13.4 Conclusion

Based on the results of the test cases, which shown a significantly positive output, future full development of the system must incorporate all the elements and include more features and modules to provide a comprehensive support application for the patient.

Table 13.1 Use case description

Use case	Description
Login	Allows patient, doctor, and admin to securely log into the application using email and password
Logout	Enables patient, doctor, and admin to safely log out the app
Add appointment	Enables patients to schedule new appointments with the gastro clinic
Manage appointment	Provides patients with the ability to view, update and delete their scheduled appointments
Add symptom	Allows patients to record and track their symptoms related to their inflammatory bowel disease (IBD) condition
View symptoms	Recorded symptoms score over time
View patients	Provides doctor and admin with a list of the clinic patients and their health information
Create consultation notes	Allows doctors to create detailed notes after each patient consultation
Manage consultation notes	Provides doctors with the ability to view, update, and delete consultation notes
Create diagnosis	Enables doctor and admin to create new diagnoses for their patients
Manage diagnosis	Provides doctor and admin with the ability to view, update, and delete diagnoses
Create test result	Allows doctor and admin to record patient's test results
Manage test results	Provides doctor and admin with the ability to view, update and delete test results
Create test result	Allows doctor and admin to record patient's test results
Manage test result	Provides doctor and admin with the ability to view, update and delete test results
View patient's concerns	Provides doctors with their patient's concerns and issues. Add medication Enables doctor and admin to prescribe and manage medications for the patients
Manage medications	Provides doctor and admin with the ability to view, update and delete prescribed medications
View resources	Offers patient access to educational resources and information about IBD.
View his own diagnoses	Allows patients to view their previous diagnoses made by their healthcare providers
View his own test results	Provides patients with access to their results related to their IBD condition
View his own Consultation notes	Allows patients to review the consultation notes provided by their doctors
View Medication	Allows patients to review their medications that prescribed by their doctor

(continued)

Table 13.1 (continued)

Use case	Description
Add resource for patients	Allows administrators to add educational resources and materials for patients
Manage resources	Provides administrators with the ability to view, update and delete resources
Create new patient's account	Enables administrators to create new patient account within the app

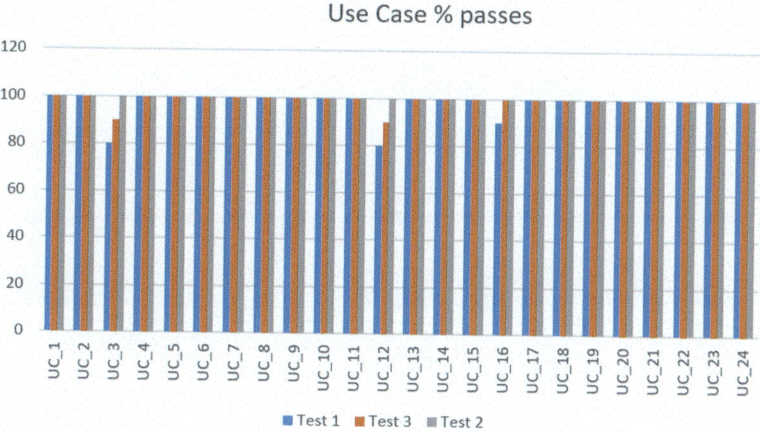

Fig. 13.3 Use test results

Acknowledgements The author would like to thank the Malaysian Institute of Information Technology, Universiti Kuala Lumpur, for the support of this research.

References

1. B. Ahmad, K. Khairatul, A. Farnaza, An assessment of patient waiting and consultation time in a primary healthcare clinic (2017). Retrieved from National Library of Medicine: https://www.ncbi.nlm.nih.gov/pmc/articles/PMC5420318/
2. H. Fauzy Yaacob, Z.N. Abu Yazid, A model of doctor-patient communication and information seeking a study among trainee or junior doctors in Malaysian hospital (2021). Retrieved from Sains Humanika: https://sainshumanika.utm.my/index.php/sainshumanika/article/view/1753/952
3. M.J. Hamilton, The use of mobile applications in the management of patients with inflammatory bowel disease (2018). Retrieved from National Library of Medicine: https://www.ncbi.nlm.nih.gov/pmc/articles/PMC6194659/

4. M. Mastronardi, M. Curlo, M. Polignano, N. Vena, D. Rossi, G. Giannelli, Remote monitoring empowerment of patients with IBDs during the SARS-CoV-2 pandemic (2020). Retrieved from National Library of Medicine: https://www.ncbi.nlm.nih.gov/pmc/articles/PMC7711761/#:~:text=Patients%20with%20IBD%20require%20constant,outcome%20and%20prevent%20further%20complications

Chapter 14
Brain Tumor Classification Using Depthwise Separable Convolution

Aifian Adi Sufian Chan, Mohammad Faiz Liew Abdullah, Saizalmursidi Md Mustam, Farhana Ahmad Poad, and Ariffuddin Joret

Abstract The number of patients diagnosed with brain tumors is on the rise. This highlights the need for a computer-assisted diagnosis system for rapid and accurate detection of brain tumors. This study has developed a lightweight model that is capable of categorizing three different classes of brain tumors. The developed model, BC-detector, uses depthwise separable convolution as the main building block. Depthwise separable convolution achieves comparable effectiveness to conventional convolutional layers while using fewer parameters. Additionally, techniques such as L2 regularization, dropout, and data augmentation were implemented to reduce the risk of overfitting. The BC-detector has obtained a high accuracy rate of more than 94% in categorizing the three classes of brain tumors and an overall accuracy of 97.39%.

Keywords Depthwise separable convolution · Image classification · Brain tumor · Convolutional neural network

A. A. S. Chan · M. F. L. Abdullah (✉) · S. M. Mustam · F. A. Poad · A. Joret
Faculty of Electrical and Electronic Engineering, Universiti Tun Hussein Onn Malaysia, Batu Pahat, Johor, Malaysia
e-mail: faiz@uthm.edu.my

A. A. S. Chan
e-mail: he200022@student.uthm.edu.my

S. M. Mustam
e-mail: saizal@uthm.edu.my

F. A. Poad
e-mail: farhana@uthm.edu.my

A. Joret
e-mail: ariff@uthm.edu.my

A. Ismail et al. (eds.), *Emerging Technologies and Sustainable Solutions*, SpringerBriefs in Applied Sciences and Technology,
https://doi.org/10.1007/978-3-032-18181-7_14

14.1 Introduction

Brain cancer, also known as a brain tumor, is currently the number one fatal cancer that is mainly prompted by cells in the brain that are uncontrolled growth [1–3]. According to the global cancer statistics in 2020 [4], there were more than 300,000 new cases of brain cancer, which accounted for 1.6% of all new cases. Moreover, brain cancer was attributed to more than 250,000 deaths, accounting for 2.5% of all cancer-related deaths. Furthermore, especially for below the age of 20 individuals, the primary cause of cancer-related deaths is brain tumors [5]. Therefore, to enhance the survival rates and optimize the effectiveness of its treatment, it is crucial to discover the cancer at an early stage [6]. When diagnosing brain tumors, magnetic resonance imaging (MRI) is the most common and reliable method due to its excellent contrast function on soft tissue [7]. MRI offers precise visualization of the brain tissue [8], improving detection. While MRI scans significantly enhance neurologists' diagnostic capabilities, the increasing patient population poses problems to the healthcare system.

Therefore, this research proposes a computer-aided diagnostic (CAD) system developed utilizing deep learning (DL) technology to assist neurologists in identifying brain tumors. The use of a computer-aided design (CAD) system can greatly enhance the diagnostic abilities of neurologists and shorten the duration of diagnosis. This enables the healthcare system to manage the continuously growing influx

Table 14.1 Image distribution in BT dataset based on type of brain tumors

Brain tumors	Number of patients	Total images	Type of view	Number of images
Glioma	91	708	Coronal	268
			Sagittal	231
			Transverse	209
Meningioma	82	930	Coronal	319
			Sagittal	320
			Transverse	291
Pituitary	60	1426	Coronal	437
			Sagittal	495
			Transverse	494
Total	233	3064	–	3064

Table 14.2 Image distribution for training and testing set

Brain tumor	Training set	Testing set	Total
Glioma	1140	286	1426
Meningioma	566	142	708
Pituitary	744	186	930
Total	2450	614	3064

Table 14.3 Techniques of data augmentation used for this research

Data augmentation techniques	Parameter setting
Range for rotation	10
Range for brightness	0.85–1.15
Range for width shift	0.002
Range for height shift	0.002
Range for shear	12.5
Horizontal flip	True

Table 14.4 Fine-tuned hyperparameter

Hyper-parameters	Parameter setting
Batch size	32
Learning rate	0.0003
Number of epochs	200
Optimizer function	Adam
Loss function	Categorical cross-entropy

Table 14.5 Proposed model testing set outcomes

Tumor type	TP	TN	FP	FN	Accuracy (%)	Precision (%)	Recall (%)	F1-score
Glioma	275	316	12	11	96.25	95.82	96.15	0.9597
Meningioma	131	466	6	11	97.23	95.62	92.25	0.9391
Pituitary	184	422	6	2	98.70	96.84	98.92	0.9787
Average scores					97.39	96.09	95.77	0.9592

Table 14.6 Comparative analysis between proposed model and previous study

Year	Approach	Accuracy (%)
2019	Using deep neural network [9]	96.13
2020	Three step hybrid approach [10]	90.27
2021	Convolutional dictionary learning with local constraint [7]	96.39
2022	Separable convolution based neural network [8]	97.52
2022	VGG16 architecture with "23 layers CNN" architecture [3]	**97.80**
–	BC-detector	97.39

of patients. The work introduced a deep learning (DL) model called BC-detector to accurately categorize brain tumors into three common forms: glioma, meningioma, and pituitary tumors [11]. The contributions of the paper are outlined below:

(i) Create a DL model with the ability to categorize three forms of brain tumors.
(ii) The DL model is lightweight and can be used with low-spec hardware.

(iii) The model introduced performed on par with and better than the previous method.

This paper is outlined as follows: Sect. 14.2 discusses the model's design and development method, whereas Sect. 14.3 showcases the study's comparative analysis. Lastly, Sect. 14.4 discusses the conclusion, limitations, and future work.

14.2 Methodology

The block diagram in Fig. 14.1 depicts the brain tumor classification into three distinct classes. The process starts with image acquisition. It uses a selected dataset for training and testing the model. The dataset is subjected to pre-processing procedures and subsequently split into two sets, that is, training and testing. The training set function is to train the model; on the other hand, the testing set evaluates its performance.

14.2.1 *Image Acquisition: Dataset and Pre-processing Procedures*

The brain tumor (BT) dataset developed by Cheng et al. [11] was used in this work. The dataset comprises MRI slices obtained from 233 patients at two different hospitals in China from 2005 to 2010. The patients were diagnosed with three forms of tumors, namely meningiomas, pituitary, and glioma tumors. Table 14.1 presents a comprehensive breakdown of the BT dataset, whereas examples of brain tumors are displayed in Fig. 14.2.

The dataset initially provided data in a MAT file with 512 × 512 image data and labels which were converted to the JPG format. Next, it undergoes pre-processing steps, which include resizing the image (150 × 150) and application of Gaussian blur. Then, the images were cropped to remove unwanted regions. Figure 14.3 shows a sample image before and after pre-processing. The dataset was randomly divided

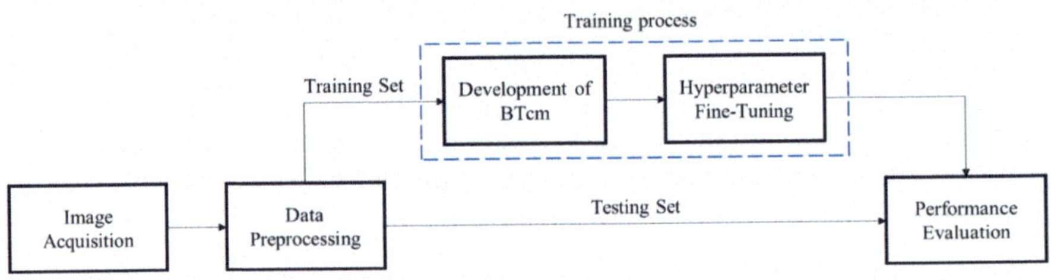

Fig. 14.1 Block diagram for the BC-detector

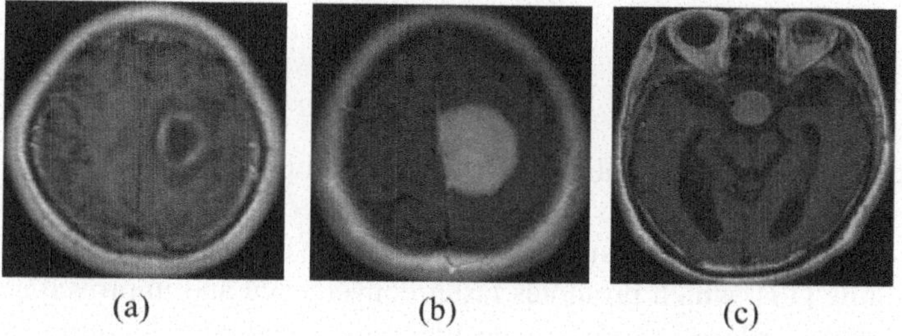

Fig. 14.2 Brain tumors consist of three types: **a** glioma; **b** meningioma; and **c** pituitary tumor

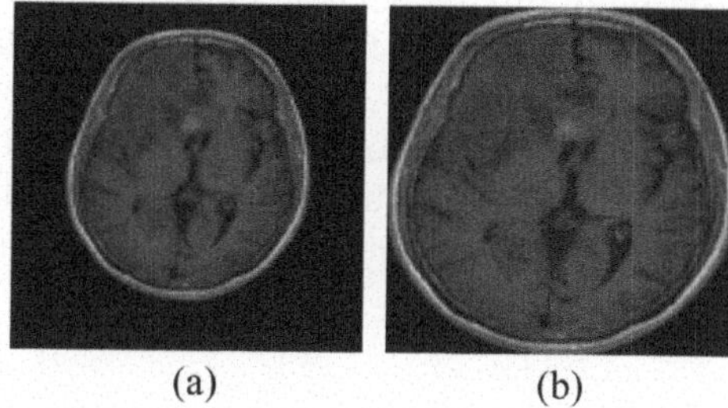

Fig. 14.3 A sample image: **a** before pre-processing; **b** after pre-processing

into test (20%) and training (80%) sets, as shown in Table 14.2. To mitigate over-fitting, data augmentation was applied to training set [12, 13] to improve the model generalization capability. The training set was diversified by utilizing various data augmentation methods listed in Table 14.3.

14.2.2 Proposed Model Architecture

The BC-detector consists of 24 layers constructed using depthwise separable convolution (DSConv). The DSConv was used due to its superior computational efficiency and reduced parameter usage in comparison to regular convolution. This layer was introduced by Chollet et al. [14] and has demonstrated its efficacy in models such as Xception [14] and GhostNet [15]. By using the DSConv as the primary component, the model becomes lightweight and efficient, enabling its deployment on low-spec devices. The BC-detector's parameter counts are under one million parameters. As an activation function, a rectified linear unit (ReLU) was proposed. The ReLU incorporates nonlinear elements so that the gradient vanishing issue is resolved during the backpropagation process. The mathematical representation is as follows:

$$F(x) = \max(0, x) \tag{14.1}$$

$$f_{\mathrm{avg}}(x) = \frac{1}{N}\sum_{i=1}^{N}|x_i| \tag{14.2}$$

The model uses average pooling (AP) to down-sample the feature map [16] where eq. 2 as depicted in Eq. 2. It uses three APs with the kernel's size and stride set to two. Batch normalization (BN) boosts model performance by using a higher learning rate during training [17], which promotes faster convergence and improved generalization. The model employed two BN layers for optimal outcomes. To mitigate the overfitting issue in a small dataset, there are two techniques being utilized. The dropout layer was implemented to randomly deactivate units [18] according to predetermined probabilities (0.35, 0.35, and 0.45). This prevents the occurrence of co-adaptation and promotes robust feature learning that leads to improved generalization of the model. Moreover, BC-detector incorporated L2 regularization, which adds a penalty term to the loss function. This encourages BC-detector to uniformly allocate weights among the features. These techniques mitigate the risk of overfitting by ensuring that the model does not excessively rely on any feature.

14.2.3 Hyperparameter Fine-Tuning

Fine-tuning hyperparameters improves the overall performance of the BC-detector [19]. Optimizing these parameters enhances the stability and speed of the training process. Table 14.4 presents the hyperparameters selected to boost the model's performance. Furthermore, early stopping was employed to mitigate overfitting and optimize time efficiency by stopping the training phase when further improvements are improbable. This strategy enhances the BC-detector's performance and ability to generalize.

14.3 Results and Analysis

This part covers the setup and comparison assessment of the BC-detector. Details regarding the hardware specifications and performance indicators for evaluation are presented. The BC-detector was evaluated in comparison to other models utilizing the test set featuring gliomas, meningiomas, and pituitary tumors.

14.3.1 Evaluation Metrics and Experimental Setup

The BC-detector was developed and evaluated using Python, TensorFlow, and Keras. The procedures were conducted on hardware using an RTX3060 GPU and 32 GB of RAM. The comparison evaluation involves four evaluation metrics, which are accuracy, recall, precision, and F1-score. Equation metrics are (3–6) as below:

$$\text{Accuracy} = \frac{\text{TP} + \text{TN}}{\text{TP} + \text{TN} + \text{FP} + \text{FN}} \tag{3}$$

$$\text{Precision} = \frac{\text{TP}}{\text{TP} + \text{FP}} \tag{4}$$

$$\text{Recall} = \frac{\text{TP}}{\text{TP} + \text{FN}} \tag{5}$$

$$\text{F}_1\text{-score} = \frac{2(\text{ Precision} \times \text{Recall})}{\text{Precision} + \text{Recall}} \tag{6}$$

Here, TP indicates true positive; FP is short for false positive; TN refers to true negative; while FN represents false negative.

14.3.2 Performance Evaluation and Analysis

Table 14.5 displays the outcomes of the BC-detector based on the four evaluation metrics when evaluated using the test set. The BC-detector demonstrates exceptional accuracy in classifying all three classes of brain tumors, resulting in an overall prediction accuracy of 97.39%. This shows that the BC-detector has the capability to achieve exceptional efficiency on the BT dataset.

The performance of the BC-detector was compared with other prior works; refer to Table 14.6. The results demonstrate that the proposed model is capable of competing with other models. The proposed framework surpasses the majority of prior studies, with the exception of the two distinct approaches presented by Isunuri et al. [8] and Khan et al. [3], respectively. The model introduced by Isunuri et al. [8] outperforms the BC-detector by a small margin of 0.13%, while the model proposed by Khan et al. [3] outperforms the proposed model by 0.41%. The slight difference in accuracy shows the model remains a suitable choice for this task. Additionally, the model is smaller than these two models. For example, the model presented by Isunuri et al. has approximately 3.4 million parameters, while the proposed model has slightly fewer than a million parameters.

14.4 Conclusion, Limitations, and Future Work

To summarize, the BC-detector was developed to categorize three distinct types of brain tumors. The model employed a 24-layer structure, primarily composed of the DSConv layer. To address the issue of overfitting, strategies such as dropout layers, L2 regularization, and data augmentation were employed. The hyperparameters were tuned to achieve the best outcomes. An evaluation conducted on a BT test set shows remarkable classification accuracy, surpassing 96% for all three categories. The overall accuracy stands at 97.39%, surpassing most prior studies but falling slightly behind models produced by Isunuri et al. [8] and Khan et al. [3].

Although the BC-detector has achieved impressive performance, it encounters a significant obstacle: a scarcity of brain tumor data. The BT dataset comprises 3064 MRI slices, encompassing solely three types among the 120 brain tumors. This hinders precise detection of brain tumors in practical scenarios. Another challenge that occurs is the intricate process of annotating brain tumors, as it requires the involvement of licensed medical professionals to ensure precise annotation. Therefore, the future goals involve the simplification and improvement of the model to make it more widely applicable on different devices. This will result in faster and safer diagnoses when a more extensive dataset is accessible.

Acknowledgements The funding for this work was provided by grant RE-GG (H884) from Universiti Tun Hussein Onn Malaysia, for which the authors are grateful.

References

1. M. Nazir, S. Shakil, K. Khurshid, Role of deep learning in brain tumor detection and classification (2015 to 2020): A review. Comput. Med. Imaging Graph. **91**, 101940 (2021). https://doi.org/10.1016/J.COMPMEDIMAG.2021.101940
2. A. Çinar, M. Yildirim, Detection of tumors on brain MRI images using the hybrid convolutional neural network architecture. Med. Hypotheses **139**, 109684 (2020). https://doi.org/10.1016/J.MEHY.2020.109684
3. M.S.I. Khan, A. Rahman, T. Debnath, M.R. Karim, M.K. Nasir, S.S. Band, A. Mosavi, I. Dehzangi, Accurate brain tumor detection using deep convolutional neural network. Comput. Struct. Biotechnol. J. **20**, 4733–4745 (2022). https://doi.org/10.1016/J.CSBJ.2022.08.039
4. H. Sung, J. Ferlay, R.L. Siegel, M. Laversanne, I. Soerjomataram, A. Jemal, F. Bray, Global cancer statistics 2020: GLOBOCAN estimates of incidence and mortality worldwide for 36 cancers in 185 countries. CA Cancer J. Clin. **71**, 209–249 (2021). https://doi.org/10.3322/CAAC.21660
5. R.L. Siegel Mph, K.D. Miller, N. Sandeep, W. Mbbs, J. Ahmedin, J. Dvm, R.L. Siegel, Cancer statistics, 2023. CA Cancer J. Clin. **73**, 17–48 (2023). https://doi.org/10.3322/CAAC.21763
6. M.K. Abd-Ellah, A.I. Awad, A.A.M. Khalaf, H.F.A. Hamed, A review on brain tumor diagnosis from MRI images: Practical implications, key achievements, and lessons learned. Magn. Reson. Imaging **61**, 300–318 (2019). https://doi.org/10.1016/J.MRI.2019.05.028
7. X. Gu, Z. Shen, J. Xue, Y. Fan, T. Ni, Brain tumor MR image classification using convolutional dictionary learning with local constraint. Front. Neurosci. **15**, 679847 (2021). https://doi.org/10.3389/FNINS.2021.679847/BIBTEX
8. B.V. Isunuri, J. Kakarla, Three-class brain tumor classification from magnetic resonance images using separable convolution based neural network. Concurrency Comput. **34**, e6541 (2022). https://doi.org/10.1002/CPE.6541
9. H.H. Sultan, N.M. Salem, W. Al-Atabany, Multi-classification of brain tumor images using deep neural network. IEEE Access. **7**, 69215–69225 (2019). https://doi.org/10.1109/ACCESS.2019.2919122

10. W. Ayadi, I. Charfi, W. Elhamzi, M. Atri, Brain tumor classification based on hybrid approach. Vis. Comput. **38**, 107–117 (2022). https://doi.org/10.1007/S00371-020-02005-1/METRICS
11. J. Cheng, W. Yang, M. Huang, W. Huang, J. Jiang, Y. Zhou, R. Yang, J. Zhao, Y. Feng, Q. Feng, W. Chen, Retrieval of brain Tumors by adaptive spatial pooling and fisher vector representation. PLoS One **11**, e0157112 (2016). https://doi.org/10.1371/JOURNAL.PONE.0157112
12. C. Shorten, T.M. Khoshgoftaar, A survey on image data augmentation for deep learning. J. Big Data **6**, 1–48 (2019). https://doi.org/10.1186/S40537-019-0197-0/FIGURES/33
13. S.Yang, W. Xiao, M. Zhang, S. Guo, J. Zhao, F. Shen, Image Data Augmentation for Deep Learning: A Survey (2022)
14. F. Chollet, Xception: Deep learning with depthwise separable convolutions. Proceedings—30th IEEE Conference on Computer Vision and Pattern Recognition, CVPR 2017.2017-January, 1800–1807 (2017). https://doi.org/10.1109/CVPR.2017.195
15. K. Han, Y. Wang, Q. Tian, J. Guo, C. Xu, C. Xu, GhostNet: More Features from Cheap Operations (2020)
16. R. Nirthika, S. Manivannan, A. Ramanan, R. Wang, Pooling in convolutional neural networks for medical image analysis: A survey and an empirical study. Neural Comput. Appl. **34**, 5321–5347 (2022). https://doi.org/10.1007/S00521-022-06953-8/TABLES/14
17. N. Bjorck, C.P. Gomes, B. Selman, K.Q. Weinberger, Understanding batch normalization. Adv Neural Inf Process. Syst. **31** (2018)
18. N. Srivastava, G. Hinton, A. Krizhevsky, I. Sutskever, R. Salakhutdinov, Dropout: A simple way to prevent neural networks from overfitting. J. Mach. Learn. Res. **15**, 1929–1958 (2014)
19. Yu, T., Zhu, H, Hyper-Parameter Optimization: A Review of Algorithms and Applications (2020)

Chapter 15
Lesson Learned from the Mox Plant Case on Precautionary Measures for Sustainable Marine Environment Management

Sumullika Dowsuwan, Rinyapath Na Songkhla, Mata Sindam, and Panuwat Pankaew

Abstract This paper aims to study the lesson learned from the Mox plant case between Ireland and England. For this case, it reflects that the International Tribunal for the Law of the Sea hereinafter ITLOS's approach of protection the marine environment under the United Nation Convention for the Law of the Sea and can be applied for the Caesiam-137 case in Thailand. The results show that in the Mox plant case, it can show and clarify the approach of prescription for provisional measure of tribunal as follows: the precautionary measures are laid down by ITLOS, the tribunal shall be considered appropriate under the circumstance to prevent serious harm to the marine environment. For this case, the tribunal prescribed the provisional measure because the Mox plant may release the radioactive material to the Irish Sea and the aforementioned cause affected the marine environment. Tribunal applies precautionary principle and takes the provisional measure to protect the environment. Additionally, these approaches of prescription of measures should be implemented by the Thai authority, Department of Industrial Works for the Caesium-137 case also. Although this Caesium case, from the inspection of state officials find that the nearby area of iron smelting plant is still safe in regard the well-being and environment. The authority should forecast the risks and effects that will happen from Caesium case by taken measures on precautionary principle as in the Mox plant case.

S. Dowsuwan (✉) · R. N. Songkhla · M. Sindam · P. Pankaew
School of Law, Thaksin University on Phatthalung Campus, Phatthalung, Thailand
e-mail: sumullika.d@tsu.ac.th

R. N. Songkhla
e-mail: rinyapath.n@tsu.ac.th

M. Sindam
e-mail: mataharees@hotmail.com

P. Pankaew
e-mail: panuwat.p@tsu.ac.th

A. Ismail et al. (eds.), *Emerging Technologies and Sustainable Solutions*, SpringerBriefs in Applied Sciences and Technology,
https://doi.org/10.1007/978-3-032-18181-7_15

Keywords Provisional measures · Mox plant · Marine environment · Caesium case

15.1 Introduction

Currently, all of the world, there are economic development by depending on natural resources and environmental factors as a main key of production. As a result, it may affect the natural resources and environment such as the impact on ecosystem, additionally, it affects the environment or marine environment. Moreover, it may be that industrial plants release waste or chemical into a river or sea. From the problems, the researcher team aims to study the preserved marine environment by lesson learned from the Mox plant case. In this case, Ireland as a plaintiff sued England to the Permanent Court of Arbitration (hereinafter PCA) under Annex VII to the Law of the Sea, 1982 (hereinafter UNCLOS). However, pending the constitution of an arbitral tribunal, Ireland requested to the International Tribunal for the Law of the Sea (hereinafter ITLOS) in order to prescript of the provisional measures as precautionary measure under legal basic [1] "in the dispute concerning the Mox plant at Sellafield in the United Kingdom, international movement of radioactive material, and the protection of the marine environment of the Irish Sea between Ireland and the United Kingdom" [2]. For that reason, if radioactive materials will be released into the sea, it affects the marine environment. Therefore, the researcher team aims to study the approach's ITLOS to save the marine environment in order to lead to sustainable management and preservation of the marine environment.

15.2 Methodology

This research is conducted by qualitative research and studying the Mox plant case and Caesium-137 Case of Thailand, by collecting relevant information from books, textbooks, articles, research papers, and the law in order to accompany this researching. Moreover, the researcher team will observe the approach's prescription provisional measures of ITLOS in order to help to protect marine environment for sustainable environment management. Additionally, the researcher will explain the observation from the Mox plant case and kick off from fact, procedural background, requesting to the tribunal, approach's prescription of precautionary measure, order of provisional measure and added value of Mox plants case that clarified protection of marine environment, respectively.

15.3 Results and Discussion

15.3.1 Fact of Mox Plant Case

On October 25, 2001, the notification was submitted by Ireland as plaintiff and the United Kingdom as respondent, filed the statement of claim to PCA. Moreover, this case, it is the dispute concerning international movement of radioactive material of the Mox plant and preservation of the marine environment of Irish Sea. The Mox plant under British Nuclear Fuels Limited (BNFL) was permitted by United Kingdom. Moreover, BNFL has operated in Sellafield, England where the area is bordering the Irish Sea [3]. However, this case, during the constitution of PCA, Ireland request to tribunal for prescription of provisional measure [4].

15.3.2 Request of State Parties

During the constitution of PCA under Annex VII, on November 20, 2001, ITLOS was requested the provisional measures by Ireland as follows:

1. That the authorization of the Mox plant will be immediately intermitted by the United Kingdom and take measures related to necessary to prevent the operation's this case;
2. That England shall secure that no movement of radioactive into the sea;
3. That England will certify that the Mox plant will not take action which might worsen, extent, cause to become more harder of situation the dispute; and.
4. That England will not take action which may unfairness the rights of Ireland related to the merit of the case under Annex VII [4].

Additionally, on the same day, ITLOS was requested by England as follows;

1. To reject the statement of claim's provisional measure of Ireland;
2. ITLOS orders that Ireland shall bear the United Kingdom's cost in this case [5].

15.3.3 Approach's Prescription of Provisional Measure

From this case, it was found that before ITLOS prescribed the measures, the first step, tribunal must take into account that if PCA have a prima facie jurisdiction, ITLOS will has jurisdiction to prescribe the precautionary measure, respectively. Furthermore, for this case, ITLOS finds prima facie jurisdiction over this case. This dispute, it is concerning the interpretation or application of law of the sea that will be considered by ITLOS. Moreover, according to article 283 of UNCLOS sets forth that "(1.) When a dispute arises between States Parties concerning the interpretation or application the convention, the parties to the dispute shall proceed expeditiously to an exchange of views regarding its settlement by negotiation of other peaceful means. (2.) The parties shall also proceed expeditiously to an exchange of views where a procedure for the settlement of such a dispute has been terminated without a settlement or where a settlement has been reached and the circumstance require consultation regarding the manner of implementing the settlement." ITLOS notes that Ireland and England proceed the exchange of view but the dispute cannot settle [5]. Moreover, researcher term notes that the approach's tribunal after finding about prima facie jurisdiction, ITLOS took into account the seriousness of situation requires the prescription of the provisional measures before constitution of PCA, respectively. However, pursuant to rule of tribunal [6], ITLOS can prescribe the precautionary measures different from requested [7] and noted provisional measure by the ITLOS as follows:

(a) The information related to the Irish Sea arising out of the commission of the Mox plant shall be exchanged between state parties;
(b) The plaintiff and defendant of this case shall cooperate in order to observe the risk of procedure of Mox plant;
(c) Disputed states shall take appropriate actions to preserve the marine environment that may arise from Mox plant.
(d) As the rule of tribunal, the initial report shall be submitted by the disputed states [8].
(e) According to legal basis [9], the plaintiff and defendant of this case shall carry its own costs [8].

This provisional measures reflects that Ireland and England as state parties of ITLOS and disputed states have a obligation to combine is a basic principle in the prevention of pollution of marine environment as the customary international law and according to statute of ICJ [10], customary international law is the one of source of international law, which has two elements as follows: firstly, state practice and secondly, opinion juris sive necessitates accepted as law that must supplement the general practice [11]. The disputed states as a party of UNCLOS shall consent to be bound under aforementioned convention. This case is one example of applying to protect the environment under precautionary principle for authority of Thailand, especially Department of Industrial Works who has directly authorized to control the pollution because Thailand has a Caesium-137 case. For this case, the Caesium disappeared from the company producing coal-fired power plants in Prachinburi province. After missing the Caesium, it was discovered and was smelted from an iron smelting plant in Prachin Buri province. However, from the inspection of state officials, the nearby area of aforementioned area is still safe [12]. For this Caesiam-137 case, the Thai authority shall take the action under the precautionary principle for protection of environment and safety for well-being of Thai people also by learned lesson from Mox plant case.

15.4 Conclusion

From the approach's prescription provisional measures of ITLOS, it can be observed that the tribunal finds prima facie jurisdiction and prescribes the provisional measure respectively. However, the provisional measure can be made without the urgency of the situation and the tribunal may make the precautionary measure relying on the precautionary principle. Moreover, this approach's prescription of provisional measure concerning protection the environment can apply for the Caesium case. Thai authority should take measure to control the smelting of Caesium based on precautionary principle for the next generation.

Acknowledgement Researcher team would like to express our special thanks of gratitude to our advisor and parent who gave us the knowledge, additionally, our dean of school of law, Thaksin University who gave the golden opportunity to do this wonderful research of lesson learned from Mox plant case on precautionary measures for sustainable marine environment management.

References

1. S. Dowsuwan, P. Onnoi, S. Thingpaktham The analysis approach's prescription of provisional measures from international tribunal for the law of the sea: case studies concerning the detention of Ukrainian naval vessels by Russia federation. 146–147 (2022)
2. V. Roeben the order the UNCLOS annex vii arbitral tribunal to suspend proceedings in the case of the MOX plant at Sellafield: how much jurisdiction subsidiarity? 223–224, (2004)
3. V. Hallum Case notes international tribunal for the law of the sea: the MOX nuclear plant case, 372 (2002)
4. International Tribunal for the Law of the Sea, https://www.itlos.org/fileadmin/itlos/documents/cases/case_no_10/published/C10-O-3_dec_01.pdf. Accessed 15 July 2022
5. International Tribunal for the Law of the Sea, https://www.itlos.org/fileadmin/itlos/documents/cases/case_no_10/published/C10-O-3_dec_01.pdf. Accessed 17 July 2022
6. S. Dowsuwan, P. Onnoi, S. Thingpaktham The analysis approach's prescription of provisional measures from international tribunal for the law of the sea: case studies concerning the detention of Ukrainian naval vessels by Russia federation, 140 (2022)
7. T. Mensah Provisional measures in the international tribunal for the law of the sea, 51 (2001)
8. International Tribunal for the Law of the Sea, https://www.itlos.org/fileadmin/itlos/documents/basic_texts/Itlos_8_E_17_03_09.pdf. Accessed 16 July 2022
9. International Tribunal for the Law of the Sea, https://www.itlos.org/fileadmin/itlos/documents/basic_texts/statute_en.pdf. Accessed 16 July 2022
10. International Court of Justice. Statute of the Court of Justice|International court of justice (icj-cij.org). Accessed 16 July 2022
11. B.S. Chimni Customary international law: a third world perpective, 2–3 (2018)
12. Prachin Buri people demand probe into caesium disappearance. www.bangkokpost.com/thailand/general/2534650/prachin-buri-people-demand-probe-into-caesium-disappearance. Accessed 15 March 2023

The manufacturer's authorised representative in the EU is Springer Nature Customer Service Centre GmbH, Europaplatz 3, 69115 Heidelberg, Germany. If you have any concerns regarding our products, please contact ProductSafety@springernature.com

Printed and bound by CPI Group (UK) Ltd, Croydon, CR0 4YY
07/07/2026
02160927-0007